D0122968

# HUMORISTS

ALSO BY PAUL JOHNSON

*Jesus: A Biography from a Believer*
*Churchill*
*Heroes*
*Creators*
*George Washington*
*Art: A New History*
*A History of the American People*
*The Quest for God*
*The Birth of the Modern*
*Intellectuals*
*A History of the English People*
*A History of the Jews*
*Modern Times*
*A History of Christianity*

# PAUL JOHNSON

# HUMORISTS

-

## From Hogarth to Noël Coward

**HARPER**

*An Imprint of* HarperCollins*Publishers*
www.harpercollins.com

HarperCollins books may be purchased for educational, business, or sales promotional use. For information, please write: Special Markets Department, HarperCollins Publishers, 10 East 53rd Street, New York, NY 10022.

FIRST EDITION

*Designed by Eric Butler*

Library of Congress Cataloging-in-Publication Data
is available upon request.

ISBN 978-0-06-182591-0

10 11 12 13 14   OV/RRD   10 9 8 7 6 5 4 3 2 1

# CONTENTS

*This book is dedicated to Blondie, Taki, and Carla,*
*who make me laugh the most.*

memoir of Liston, but the player outlived him: he was able to retire at sixty and died ten years later, in 1846, a rich man.

But Lamb's favorite comic was Joseph Munden, and he wrote about him often (so did the author and artist William Hazlitt). Indeed, Lamb's "Autobiography of Mr. Munden," printed in the *London Magazine* in 1825, an imaginary pastiche which imitates his stage mannerisms, vocabulary, and stutters, and seems to convey even the tone of voice, is one of the best things he ever did. Lamb says he was a remarkably funny baby, and had them all laughing at his christening— even the vicar tittered over the font. Lamb liked this, for he himself often laughed surreptitiously in church—"Anything awful makes me laugh. I was once almost expelled from a funeral." But Lamb, well acquainted with misery himself— there was madness in his family, and his beloved sister, his lifetime companion, had murdered their mother—was aware of the Yorick syndrome of melancholy, which gets most comedians in its grip. Lamb described the case of James William Dodd, who played Shakespeare's Aguecheek brilliantly, and the society fops of John Dryden and Richard Brinsley Sheridan— "the most perfect fopping ever placed upon the English stage," he wrote—whom he once came across alone and meditating in the garden of Gray's Inn. Dodd was a well-educated, even learned, man, whose collection of Elizabethan literature was famous and eagerly bought by erudite bibliophiles when auctioned after his death. In a fine passage in his essay "On Some of the Old Actors," Lamb contrasts Dodd's jovial excursions on the stage with his serious mien in the Inn garden:

Was this the face—manly, sober, intelligent—which I had so often despised, made mocks at, made merry with? The remembrance of the freedoms which I had taken with it came upon me with a reproach of insult. I could have asked it pardon. I thought it looked upon me with a sense of injury. There is something strange as well as sad in seeing actors—your pleasant fellows particularly—subject to, and suffering, the common lot—their fortunes, their casualties, their deaths, seem to belong to the scene, their actions to be amenable to poetic justice only. We can hardly connect them with more awful responsibilities. The death of this fine actor took place shortly after this meeting. He had quitted the stage some months; and as I learned afterwards, had been in the habit of resorting daily to these gardens almost to the day of his decease. In these serious walks probably he was divesting himself of many scenic and some real vanities—weaning himself from the frivolities of the lesser and the greater theatre— doing gentle penance for a life of no very reprehensible fooleries—taking off by degrees the buffoon mask which he might feel he had worn too long—and rehearsing for a more solemn cast of part.

Actors, to be sure, are only one category in the professional business of making the world laugh, even if they are the most important one. There are also writers, especially playwrights, novelists, poets, and even essayists like Lamb (and myself). There are painters, draftsmen, and cartoonists. Even musi-

# INTRODUCTION

W. C. FIELDS, WHO spent sixty years trying to amuse people on stage, in print, on the airwaves, in silent movies and talkies, put his finger on it: "We know *what* makes people laugh. We do not know *why* they laugh." Laughter is like dreams. We know as much about it now as we did five thousand years ago, and no more. About 2900 BC, in ancient Egypt, a hieroglyph for "laugh" or "laughing" appeared. It went like this:

Sir Alan Gardiner, who knew more about ancient Egypt than anyone else, who compiled an *Egyptian Grammar*, and who had a beautiful hand for these majestic squiggles, said, "Whenever I write that hieroglyph, I find myself laughing." "Why, Sir Alan?" "Oh, I don't know, Old Boy. Thinking of those funny old priests, chipping it into the rock."

The Old Testament contains twenty-six laughs, which do not form any particular pattern or expand our knowledge of why people laugh. The first occurs in chapter 18 of the book of Genesis, and is the first time a case of laughter was recorded in words, about 1500 BC. Abraham is sitting outside his tent. Angels appear, one of whom turns out to be God. Abraham sends his wife Sarah scurrying back into the tent to prepare a meal for his guests. God gives Abraham the astounding news: " 'Lo! Sarah, thy wife, shall have a son.' And Sarah heard it in the tent door, which was behind him. Now Abraham and Sarah were old and well stricken in age; and it ceased to be with Sarah after the manner of women. Therefore Sarah laughed within herself, saying, 'After I am waxed old shall I have pleasure, my lord, being old also?' "

God was affronted by Sarah's laugh, thinking it a reflection on His powers: "Is anything too hard for the Lord?" Then Sarah denied laughing, saying, " 'I laughed not': for she was afraid." And God said, "Nay but thou didst laugh."

This little episode from Genesis is so fascinating that it makes one believe in the Bible as an authentic record. It is not only the first recorded joke but also the first "dirty joke"— Sarah laughs not at the idea of a baby but at the idea of intercourse with her Old Man, and achieving orgasm ("have pleasure"). What, would Abraham get an erection again? It seemed unlikely, did it not? And therefore Sarah's laugh was skeptical; it was also ironic, not to say sardonic. As such, very irritating to the all-powerful deity.

The incident shows that there is no such thing as a simple laugh. I am tempted to add: or an innocent laugh. The commonest occasion of laughter, especially collective laughter, is the distress, perplexity, or discomfiture of others. God himself does not laugh in the Old Testament, but the pagan gods of Homer laugh repeatedly in the *Iliad*. As Matthew Arnold puts it in "Empedocles on Etna," "The gods laugh in their sleeve / to watch man doubt and fear." And that relentless philosopher Thomas Hobbes, translating a line of Homer (*Iliad* 1.561), comes up with: "And then the gods laugh all at once, outright—at man's peril." No wonder that he produced, in *Leviathan*, the definition that "the passion of laughter is nothing else but sudden glory arising from a sudden conception of some eminence in ourselves by comparison with the infirmity of others, or with our own formerly."

In the English language, the attempts of people, from the earliest times, to record laughter in words meant that there were large numbers of different ways of spelling the word: the *Oxford English Dictionary* records thirty-six. King Alfred had a go in 897. Chaucer, in 1385, in his prologue to *The Legend of Good Women*, got it almost correct: "Ryght so move ye oute of myn hert bringe switch vois, right as yow lyst, to laughe or pleyne," a line so lovely as to make the senses tingle. So far as we can see, Shakespeare wrote it different ways, his favorite being "loffe," perhaps reflecting Warwickshire pronunciation. This occurs in some unfeeling but riotous lines of Puck in *A*

*Midsummer Night's Dream,* usually omitted from most productions as too vulgar:

> And sometimes lurk I in a gossip's bowl
> In very likeness of a roasted crab.
> And when she drinks, against her lips I bob,
> And on her withered dewlap pour the ale.
> The wisest aunt, telling the saddest tale,
> Sometimes for three-foot stool mistaketh me;
> Then slip I from her bum, down topples she,
> And "tailor" cries, and falls into a cough;
> And then the whole quire hold their hips and loffe.

The fall must have hurt, and the fact that "the whole quire" laughed at the old woman's pain must have made it worse, so here is a case, all too common, of laughter being aggressive and cruel. Max Beerbohm, himself adept at amusing, thought that "there are two elements in the public's humor: delight in suffering, contempt for the unfamiliar"—one reason people laugh at foreigners or strangers generally. Both motives are reprehensible. Laughter, when you analyze it, is no joke. One of the best essays on the subject I know is in that usually dull tome, the modern *Encyclopaedia Britannica,* and was written by Arthur Koestler—who is no joke either, having ended his melancholy life not merely by committing suicide but by persuading his much younger and more cheerful mistress to do likewise. Koestler argues that there is usually something nasty about a

laugh, irrespective of the level of sophistication of those enjoying it. Thus he instances the very primitive Bushmen of the
Kalahari Desert of South Africa. What really makes them roar
is when a springbok, fatally wounded by a bullet, continues to
jump and kick in its death agony. He describes laughing as a
"luxury reflex," containing elements of aggression and hostility, even savagery, as well as humor. This accords with the view
of Henri Bergson, the French-Jewish philosopher, who wrote a
famous tract on the subject, later published as a book, *Le rire*.
"In laughter," he wrote, "we always find an unavowed intention to humiliate and so to correct our neighbor." In particular, he added, mirth was "the collective punishment of society
on the unsociable individual."

I think this last point may be more true of France than of
England or America. Jean-Paul Sartre told me in 1953 that
his ability to make people laugh "saved my life" at school. He
said, "I was small, ugly, no good at games, not much good at
lessons because my eyesight was so poor. They said I smelt too,
and maybe I did. But I could make them laugh. What I found
was that it was easier to make a lot of them laugh, than just
one of them. And the laughter was louder if I could direct it
at a single little boy, even more miserable and friendless than I
was. So that's what I did." "And is it the same principle in the
theatre, Maître?" "Of course. *Absolument*."

There have been many attempts to analyze the physical side
of laughter, especially in antiquity and in the Renaissance,
indeed right up to the end of the nineteenth century. Charles

Lamb's friend Thomas Holcroft, who dabbled in this field, wrote, "The physiognomy of laughter would be the best of elementary books for the knowledge of man." Personally, I doubt it. Herbert Spencer, as one would expect, had an elaborate theory about emotions, including risibility, being translated into bodily movements. It was taken up by Freud, who agreed that such emotion was repressed: in relief from tension, "the muscles of the smile follow the line of least resistance, so laughter is a form of respiratory gymnastics." And here is Koestler again: "Laughter is a trigger-release, detonating vast amounts of stored emotions, derived from various, often unconscious sources: repressed sadism, sexual tumescence, unavowed fear, even boredom." He drew attention to the explosive laughter of a group of schoolboys, in class, at a trivial detonator, usually a word with some hidden sexual connotation. My memories of boarding school are that such words as "mutual" (code for mutual masturbation), "bishop" (description of the head of a penis), and "windy" (obscurely derived from the Americanism "blow job," itself a mystery to do with whaling), could set the class on a roar—to the intense irritation of the master, needless to say, who reacted like God to Sarah's laughter.

Many people, for a variety of reasons, hate to hear others laugh. Although the pun is as old as Homer, and probably older (though I have yet to find one in hieroglyphics), it has always had dedicated enemies. Karl Marx thought to pun was a sure sign of "the intellectual *lumpen proletariat*," and rebuked Engels for so lowering himself (in German, of course). Jeremy Bentham thought punning "an atrocity." But few will resist a pun if they have the wit to make a good one. Milton, not normally thought of as a humorist, had a pun when dealing with the ravens who fed Elijah: "The birds, though ravenous, [were] taught to abstain from what they brought." There is also a suspect pun in the way the elephant "with the lithe proboscis" entertained Adam and Eve on their first evening together, in *Paradise Lost*. Even Freud stooped to punning, referring to the Christmas season as "the alcoholidays." Lamb regarded punning as one of the great tripods of life's pleasures, the other two being smoking and drinking gin. He said he hoped that "the last breath I draw in this world will be through a pipe, and exhaled in a pun." Max Eastman, in his book *The Enjoyment of Laughter*, takes a dim view of punning. He says of one Ogden Nash effort, "It is not a pun: it is a punitive expedition." But that is a pun too. Groucho Marx said to me, "For a professional comedian to fall back on a pun is a confession of failure, like telling a dirty joke." But he was the man who, asked about his safari in Kenya, replied, "We shot two bucks. That was the only money we had."

Some people have always refused to laugh at puns, even if inclined to. But then some people are disinclined to laugh at anything. Morecambe and Wise, the famous team of Northern comedians, used to complain about the propensity of Yorkshire audiences to "zip their teeth up," as they put it. Eric Morecambe claimed one man in Leeds said to him, "Ee, lad, thou wert so funny tonight I almost had to laff." Those who refuse to laugh have different reasons for their obduracy. Philip Dormer Stanhope, fourth earl of Chesterfield, the self-appointed arbiter of eighteenth-century taste, thought laughing was vulgar, though a smile was permissible. Horace Walpole (fourth earl of Orford) found laughing men, such as the painter William Hogarth, offensive. Lord Chatham thought laughing impermissible for a gentleman: it belonged to the lower orders. Jane Austen did not go so far but evidently, as episodes in both *Sense and Sensibility* and *Pride and Prejudice* indicate, regarded that the way in which a person laughed indicated whether he was fit for polite society or she was a lady.

But these were social points or distinctions. In Germany, as in parts of Yorkshire, laughing—at least among people with pretensions to rank—was regarded as a form of weakness. Goethe, whose own laughter was seldom observed, thought a lady might laugh where a gentleman should keep a straight face. Frederick the Great might laugh with a Frenchman, such as Voltaire, but "would not so condescend" with his compatriots. Field Marshall Helmuth von Moltke, the leading nineteenth-century Prussian strategist, was said to have laughed only twice: once when told that a certain French fortress was impregnable, and once when his mother-in-law died. Martin Heidegger, whom some regard as the greatest philosopher of the twentieth century but many find incomprehensible, was even more sparing of his mirth. He is recorded to have laughed only once, at a picnic with Ernst Jünger in the Harz Mountains. Jünger leaned over to pick up a sauerkraut and sausage roll, and his lederhosen split with a tremendous crack. Heidegger let out a shout of glee, but immediately checked himself, "and his facial expression reverted to its habitual ferocity." The more strait-laced Germans were prepared to laugh provided they did so briefly. Before the First World War, the commanding officer of the Death's Head regiment of Hussars, then the smartest in the Prussian army, became concerned about the way his sub-alterns were laughing. He called a meeting in the mess ante-room of all officers below the rank of captain, and said, "You young officers are laughing in a way I do not like, or permit. I do not wish to hear from you sniggers, titters or guffaws. You are not tradespeople, Jews or Poles. There is only one way in which a cavalry officer may laugh: short, sharp and manly. Thus: Ha! Do you hear, *Ha*! Nothing else will be tolerated. Now, I want to hear you all practice it. One, two, three, *Ha*! Come along there! One, two, three, *Ha*! One, two, three, *Ha*! That's better. Now, once again, all together, One, two, three, *Ha*! Practice it among yourselves. Dismiss!"

"It is a fact," wrote Stephen Spender, after trying to write a book about interwar Berlin, "that all the best German jokes are unconscious." He instanced the expostulation of the German conductor Hans Richter, after a difficult rehearsal with the London Philharmonic Orchestra: "Up with your damned nonsense will I put twice, or perhaps once, but sometimes always, by God, never!"

Accidental humor is perhaps the best, and particularly welcome, since making people laugh by the exercise of profes-sional skills is, and always has been, hard work; expensive too and requiring organization. The Greek city-states inherited a tradition of professional humor from the Hittites, and in all the cities of the *oikoumene*, the area of Greek civilization, there were permanent theaters, where comedies as well as tragedies were enacted, and where clowns, tumblers, acrobats, and other skilled professionals performed. Republican Rome had theaters too, but under the empire the chief employer of professional talent was the court. This tradition was resurrected when Christian Europe began to emerge from the gloomiest period of the Dark Ages. In England, the Anglo-Saxon kings had expert jesters and songmakers to amuse them. So did the Normans and, still more, the Plantagenet rulers, and we know the names of some of these laugh-makers, and what they were paid.

However, it was in the early Tudor period, 1485 to 1547, that the business of professional entertainment came of age in England. It centered around the Office of the Revels. It is curious that this department of state should have been founded by King Henry VII, a dour, unsmiling man who had spent much of his life in exile, had won his throne by force at the desperate battle of Bosworth, and had then had to defend it for the rest of his weary days from plotters and insurgents. He was never known to smile, let alone laugh. His main task in life was to restore the national finances, and this he did in good measure: his initials can be seen at the bottom of every page of the royal accounts, signifying that he examined, checked, and approved of each line.

However, he must have thought it was part of his kingly duty to provide entertainment at his courts. So the Revels Office was set up in the mid-1490s, and thereafter it was the center of the English professional entertainment industry. The master of the revels varied, for this was a high court post held by a member of the aristocracy. But the real power in the office was held by a permanent official named Richard Gibson. He knew his job. He had been an actor, and the producer-manager of a group called the King's Players. He held many jobs: porter of the wardrobe, where all the royal clothes, for both the men and the women, for ceremonial occasions were kept, and also its yeoman tailor, responsible for producing new clothes, as the occasion required. In addition he was sergeant of tents, in charge of the mobile sleeping-quarters when the court was on the move, being in due course promoted to be pavilionary, designing the immense royal tents needed for occasions of special display. It was Gibson who thought of the idea of a special summit conference between Henry VIII and Francis I of France, the first such occasion in history. Or rather, it was Gibson who made it possible by providing pavilions on such a scale of sumptuousness that the event, in 1520, was thereafter known as the Field of the Cloth of Gold. It was a great extravaganza, which no one present ever forgot, with jousting, plays, concerts, parades, fireworks, feasts, and twenty-four-hour drinking, the wine spouting from special fountains designed by the mechanics of the Revels Office. It was so expensive it was never repeated, but Gibson goes down in history as the first true international impresario, a line which stretches across the centuries to include Sergei Diaghilev in the years of the Ballets Russes, just before the First World War. It is not known whether Gibson ever made a joke himself. But he provided the physical setting in which he enabled others to do so, and he hired all the stars. One of the men he engaged to do the decorative work was Hans Holbein the Younger, the greatest painter in northern Europe. So Gibson knew how to pick them.

Gibson kept very detailed financial accounts in his execrable handwriting. So we know he paid £1 2s. for a "device to make thunder and lightning," that he bought masks and "vizards" for £4 5s., and paid the large sum of £6 16s. to a "wire drawer," a key craftsman in the construction of gilded scene-effects. He ensured that the theatrical "stuff" was periodically "aired" as well as "safeguarded." He also cracked down on the habit of underlings who earned money by hiring out royal fancy dress to "lords, lawyers and citizens." This and much else can be seen in the Public Record Office in London, or more easily read in E. K. Chambers's masterpiece *The Elizabethan Stage*, published in four volumes in 1923. I dwell on these details to make the point that behind the laughter of the ages are dull, industrious little men who made all possible, and well-run organizations which provided the platform. The Elizabethan stage did not spring out of nothing—it was ultimately the product of the Revels Office, progenitor of the companies and theaters in which Shakespeare was able to display his genius.

No man ever provided more occasions for laughter than Shakespeare, and laughter of all kinds too: uproarious clowning and farce, horseplay and tumbling, sardonic jests and subtle jests, coterie in-jokes, wit both sly and majestic, and the mockery of human infirmity of every kind. He was helped by all kinds of experts, like Edward Alleyn, the L. B. Mayer or Cecil B. De Mille of his day, and great actors like Richard Burbage, who did his Othello and Hamlet and Lear. But equally important, perhaps more important, in terms of the "groundlings," was his chief funny man, Richard Tarlton. Tarlton was an amazing fellow. He had all the skills of the traditional jester. He could juggle. He could sing, and write his songs and compose the music. He was an expert fencer, and constructed a fencing act which raised tremendous laughter, especially when he performed it with Elizabeth I's little dog, Perrico. He could dance "on his toes" like a modern ballet dancer. The music for some of his jigs still exists, and the texts of things he wrote, such as *The Seven Deadly Sins*. He interpreted Shakespeare's comic roles from his early work but was also a stand-up comic, who could ad-lib and compose extemporaneous recitals, taking in the current news of the town. The queen loved his chatter until he went too far, making nasty cracks about one of her favorites, Sir Walter Raleigh, who was unpopular as a monopoly holder. Worse, he "reflected on the overgreat power and riches of the Earl of Leicester," her top courtier. So "she forbad Tarlton and all her jesters from coming near her table, being inwardly displeased with this impudent and unseasonable liberty." So there was a family row over his will, something (as we shall see) which often provides a sad commentary on the lives of funny men. "Alas, poor Yorick!" as Shakespeare said.

Shakespeare was the first man not only to make jokes but to write movingly, and illuminatingly, of those who did it for a living. The eulogy of Yorick which he put into the mouth of Hamlet in the graveyard scene is a milestone. The monumental nature of this speech was very clear to Charles Lamb, and he showed his gratitude to Shakespeare for his example by writing admirably of the comics who strode the stage in his own day. He identified one of the most powerful instruments of mirth used by the professional comedian—the catchphrase, invented in the eighteenth century and still very much in use today. In the case of Dicky Suett, one of his favorites, it was the catch-laugh: "Ha, ha, ha! Ho, ho, ho—Oh La!" Lamb adds, "He drolled upon the stock of those two syllables richer than the cuckoo."

Lamb was particularly admiring of the laugh-raising talents of John Liston, who began as a tragic actor, failed, then switched to comedy, and was so funny he became the first comic "to command a salary higher than a tragedian." As a person, he was never known to smile. Indeed in private life he was melancholic—a common trait of professional jokers—and addicted to theology. He had a weird, long, lugubrious face, and had only to appear on stage, and illuminate his mug over the footlights, to set people laughing. That too is the way of the true comic. My old acquaintance Frankie Howerd said to me, "My visage is my most precious possession. It brings me nothing but grief in the shaving mirror but one glimpse of it by the paying public sets them a-tittering." A quiet man, not given to drinking or roistering, Liston was always at work, and well looked after by his tiny, plump, twinking doll-wife. He was a practical joker, a wit, and a punster, competing with Lamb, his friend, for the most outrageous. Lamb wrote a cod cians, though making people laugh by musical means in a concert or opera, is not easy; impossible as a rule. We smile at the last ten bars of Richard Strauss's *Der Rosenkavalier* when the page retrieves the handkerchief to an inspired orchestral accompaniment, but we do not laugh. Still less do attempts by composers to imitate noises, as in Beethoven's *Pastoral* Symphony or during the longueurs of Wagner's *Nibelungenlied*, make us guffaw. And it is certainly not the business of an architect, though some now attempt it at great expense, normally the public's, thus strengthening the justice of Auberon Waugh's assertion that "all architects should be executed on principle."

This last remark gives us a useful entry into the business of humor. No one seriously supposes that all architects should be subjected to the death penalty. At least I think not, though it is conceivable that Adolf Hitler, who took architecture more seriously than anyone else in his time, might (had he won the war) have introduced capital punishment for architects he disapproved of. All the same, the idea of catastrophe overtaking the creators of vast monstrosities is funny, and appealing. It is anarchic, but agreeable. Here we come across one of the central forces which produces laughter, in the same way that disturbance in the bowels of the earth leads to earthquakes, geysers, tidal waves, and avalanches. The force is chaos, contemplated in safety.

Comics who create chaos form one of the main categories of those examined in this volume: Hogarth and Thomas Rowlandson, for instance, W. C. Fields, Laurel and Hardy,

Groucho Marx, Evelyn Waugh, and James Thurber. There are many different kinds of chaos, and a great variety of ways in which chaos can be created: therein lies the art. And there are those who, while not chaos-creators as such, recognize recondite forms of it, and relish it, such as Dorothy Parker who, on opening a door into a crowded room, feels impelled to ask, "What fresh Hell is this?"—the accent being on *fresh*. On the other hand, there are those who look for, and find, and analyze, the worrying exuberance, and sheer egregious weirdness of the individual human being, and who present them vividly and accurately for our delight. Among such, another wide category in this book, are Toulouse-Lautrec and George Bernard Shaw, Damon Runyon and Dickens, G. K. Chesterton and, again, Evelyn Waugh, who switches to this mode of humor in his later novels, though twitches of chaos still ruffled the deep waters of his prose. Of course, in addition to these two principal categories, there are other powerful sources of humor, especially categorization, that is the interplay between different classes, races, nationalities, and ages. Hence we find specialists such as Noël Coward, Charlie Chaplin (though he was also an expert on chaos), P. G. Wodehouse, and Nancy Mitford. Today, of course, being an age of Political Correctness, the increasingly authoritarian form of militant liberalism, many types of this kind of humor are censored, indeed some are unlawful and punished by prison sentences. But it is the fate of the comedian to court danger, and the more funny he or she is, the more likely is jail or the execution shed. But if comics fall into broad categories, each, if any good, is sui generis. The gallery I have assembled in this book is a strange collection of geniuses, worldly failures, drunks, misfits, cripples, and gifted idiots. They had in common only the desire, and the ability, to make large numbers of people laugh. In this series of books collecting together intellectuals, creators, and heroes, I reckon the comics are the most valuable. The world is a vale of tears, always has been and surely always will be. Those who can dry our tears, and force reluctant smiles to trembling lips, are more precious to us, if the truth be told, than all the statesmen and the generals and brainy people, even the great artists. For they ease the agony of life a little, and make us even imagine the possibility of being happy. And as Dickens's Mrs. Gamp says, "What a blessed thing it is—living in a wale—to be contented."

CHAPTER ONE

# HOGARTH: THE GRAND OLD MASTER OF CHAOS

WILLIAM HOGARTH (1697–1764) is the only great master to make you laugh: not just once or twice but often, regularly, consistently, at first glance, and in retrospect. Moreover, the closer you look at his work, the more you laugh. To get the best out of him, as Charles Lamb observed in his essay on Hogarth—the neatest thing ever written on the subject—you must not only look at his work, but *read* it. Indeed study it. Lamb enjoyed his prints so much that he stuck them up on the walls in his home. He had a whole room devoted to Hogarth, the place covered in prints, from floor to ceiling, which he furnished with a ragged old carpet and a rackety easy chair; and there he would sit, and drink gin, and smoke his pipe, and laugh.

Hogarth often observed, and Lamb certainly agreed with him, that making people laugh was hard work. He always worked hard himself. He had to. Life and livelihood, to him, never came easy, from birth to death. His father was an ambitious autodidact from the north of England, who had nothing more than a grammar school education but became a passable classical scholar. He came south to set up a school but lacked the capital to make it work. He compiled a Latin dictionary but was cheated and bamboozled by rascally bookseller-publishers, of whom there were plenty in eighteenth-century London. So he opened a coffeehouse, whose feature was that everyone there was expected to speak Latin. There was a huge table in the middle covered in pamphlets, with men sitting around, leaning on their elbows, and learning. A good idea, and popular, but not profitable, and since old Hogarth had borrowed money to set it up, he was arrested, marched into a "sponging house," and spent the last few years of his life in debtors' prison.

This tragedy overshadowed Hogarth's early life (as it did for Dickens exactly a century later), but it did not deter him from upward striving. He was just as ambitious as his father, and wanted to be a great man. But he was much more cautious, and realistic. He never borrowed a penny unless he absolutely had to. He never trusted anyone. He ran his own affairs, was his own master in all things, paid cash, saved his money, and acquired basic business skills. He was determined to be an artist, for he loved drawing and got some lessons in painting at an academy in St. Martin's Lane, off Leicester Fields. He also, to ensure he made a living and could pay his bills, got himself apprenticed to an engraver and learned this difficult craft thoroughly. He was thus able to engrave all his own works, until he was successful enough to employ the best Paris engravers, who had a sophisticated touch then unknown in London. Always he was overshadowed by the fear of prison, which often makes an appearance in his works, sometimes openly, more often by implication, as a threat just around the corner. It was his lifelong terror that he would end up as his father did.

But he had one stroke of superb luck. He went to work for Sir James Thornhill, the muralist, who without being a genius was a thorough professional who taught Hogarth a lot, and was industrious, workmanlike, and helpful in all things. Moreover, he had a beautiful daughter, Jane, who was also highly intelligent and understood business thoroughly, and he fell in love with her. She returned his love, but old Thornhill was opposed at first, thinking Hogarth a nobody. However, at Jane's strenuous urging, he looked carefully into Hogarth's work, working hours, and productivity, and decided "he will do." They made a perfect couple, for Jane loved his work and helped him in every way she could. She sat for him on many occasions, notably as the kneeling woman in his first success-ful picture, a scene from the hit play *The Beggar's Opera*, as the tempted lady in *The Lady's Last Stake*, and above all (I believe) as *The Shrimp Girl*, the superb oil sketch which has become his most popular work. His sense of humor was hers too, and she said, "Mr. Hogarth loves to laugh, and he has taught the world to laugh with him." After his death she kept his flame burning steadily by organizing the sales of his paintings and the reissue of his prints. She was the perfect wife for the professional man, and I salute her. Hogarth was also fortunate in that he is the subject of two of the best essays in the English language, by Lamb and Hazlitt; and in our own time, the American scholar Ronald Paulson has devoted to him the best three-volume biography written about any eighteenth-century Englishman (see Further Reading section).

Hogarth was one of the most versatile artists in history. His work includes large- and small-scale murals, individual and group portraits, conversation pieces, historical paintings, and studies of modes and manners. Some of his self-portraits are masterpieces, especially his own favorite, showing himself and his pug, which brings out their affinity. He was himself, as he said, "dogged"; also brave, tenacious, and faithful, and he looked the part. He was widely known as Pug or Puggy, and was proud of it. He liked similarly pugnacious characters, and his best portraits are of such people: Benjamin Hoadly, bishop of Winchester; Thomas Herring, archbishop of Canterbury; the Welsh mathematician William Jones of the Royal Society; Captain Thomas Coram, who set up the Foundling Hospital in London (which still exists as a museum that houses some of Hogarth's best work); and even a pugnacious woman, Mrs. Salter, one of the finest and most truthful presentations of an ordinary lady we possess. Hogarth's small-scale portrait of the successful merchant George Arnold is the quintessence of the self-confident spirit of independence which was so characteristic of the mid-eighteenth century. These works are not exactly funny. But they make one smile; they are so truthful to unadorned humanity. They can be moving too: Hogarth's portrait-heads of his six servants on the same canvas is a virtuoso exercise in gentle and generous truth telling.

However, the core of Hogarth's work is his moral paintings, in which he sought to tell the truth about English society in the hope of reforming it. It was his view that the truth is both tragic and comic, and both aspects are essential. In order to direct his moral message at the largest possible public, he usually presented it in a series of connected images, a story, first painted (for sale to wealthy individual collectors), then engraved (usually by himself) for mass sale in the print shops. The central characters are usually tragic, the peripheral ones comic. Sometimes the story is told in two images, more often in four or six. Thus, in *Gin Lane* and *Beer Street* (unusual in that it was never painted but went straight into engraved form), he contrasts the evils of cheap gin with the healthy normality of English beer. In *Before and After*, he shows an ardent lover striving purposefully to have sexual intercourse with a reluctant, but also excited, maid; and the disarray, both in their clothing and emotions, after he has succeeded. There is nothing objectively funny in either of these two pairs, indeed *Gin Lane* contains much that is tragic, even horrible, and the seduction pair suggests much trouble ahead for both parties as a result of their surrender to passion or lust. But we get great humorous pleasure from both: from their humanity, jovial truthfulness, and confidentiality. We are glad to see what is happening, and glad it is not happening to us; so we can laugh in safety. The safe laugh at the expense of a sad world is one of the chief effects a professional humorist seeks to bring about, and it was Hogarth's principal strength.

His grand stories number four: *Times of Day, A Harlot's Progress, A Rake's Progress,* and *Marriage à-la-mode.* On these his fame principally rests. With them, he founded an English school of painting, and they have become part of the English artistic heritage. The four *Times, Morning, Noon, Evening,* and *Night,* are essentially street scenes, with realistic urban or suburban backgrounds, and an immense variety of characters: bucks and their floozies, screaming and unhappy children, negligent buxom servants having their breasts stroked and so pouring the dishes they carry on to the street, sweating middle-aged women, rheumatic old men, censorious old maids, and gawkers, mendicants, tradesmen, even barbers shaving. Hogarth manages to convey cold, greed, anger, jealousy, envy, and lust as part of the everyday experience of Londoners on the streets. It is an early work (1738) and the painting is sometimes crude. But it is also forceful, direct, uncompromising, and driven forward with single-minded energy. The images strike home and imprint themselves on the mind. It is fierce human comedy—no punches pulled—but we can laugh: we are not in the streets, shivering or broiling, or having hot soup poured on our heads, but safe at home, chuckling.

*A Harlot's Progress* has a central character, a country maid, being seduced into vice by a procuress, throwing away her chances of wealth by intemperate behavior, being arrested for debt, doing hard labor in prison, and finally ending up in her coffin. It is a six-scene series of sustained power and brilliance, in which the structure of center-tragic, periphery-comic is brought to maturity, especially in the finale. Here, with the harlot in her open coffin, there are fourteen characters in the room, all theoretically mourners but none caring tuppence for the dead woman, and enjoying themselves or acting their grief with varying degrees of humbug. The key character is the parson, sitting next to a handsome woman. His face expresses piety but his right hand has strayed under her skirts and is feeling her naked thigh. She does not give him away but directs at the viewer a glance of complicity, as if to say, "What a hypocrite this dreadful old clergyman is." This comic device, which I call the Complicity Stare, in which the participant communes directly with the viewer/reader, was well-known on the stage, going back to Shakespeare. But this is the first time it is used in European pictorial art, and is a scintillating debut. It was to have a great future, not only in graphic humor but, more important, in the cinema, where Oliver Hardy brought it to perfection in his silent shorts. In this case, the parson's misbehavior is not just a secret between himself and the lady he is fingering. An old woman on his left has noticed what he is up to, and is scowling horribly. Maybe she is about to make a fuss and expose him. Hogarth at his best not only tells you what has just happened, but suggests what is about to happen, so the viewer is present at a moment in time of a dynamic story.

*A Harlot's Progress* was painted in 1731, but the canvases

were destroyed by fire in 1755, and only the prints, from 1732, remain. They were a huge success and Hogarth followed up the series in 1734 with *A Rake's Progress*, eight painted scenes, now in Sir John Soane's Museum, which also went into print form—Hogarth, for the first time, feeling rich enough to get the help of a French engraver, Louis Gerard Scotin. It is more sophisticated that the *Harlot* series, and scene 3, *The Rake at the Rose Tavern*, a brothel-cum-inn in Drury Lane, is one of Hogarth's masterpieces. Here, for the first time, he paints a scene of carefully contrived chaos, with the Rake, drunk and being robbed, as central character, and the whores grouped around him in various acts of depravity. There is a great deal to look at, examine in detail, speculate about, and laugh at— including a lubricious activity involving a candle and a mirror. Thereafter follows his arrest for debt, his marriage in desperation to a rich widow, his ruin in a gambling house, his incarceration, and finally his death in Bedlam. These are somber matters, painted with severity but also with compassion, horrible but (I fear) funny too. In the Bedlam scene, which Hogarth composed after making sketches in the madhouse, the realism is overpowering, not least the two society ladies coming to see the antics of the lunatics as a treat, and obviously getting their money's worth. Hogarth cuts near the bone, but the humor, however dark, is still there.

*Marriage à-la-mode*, the most popular of the moral series tales, at the time and since, shows what happens when the heir of an impoverished nobleman marries the daughter of a rich businessman, for convenience. Every episode has its outstanding qualities, but the one in which the husband discovers his wife in adultery with her lover, and is mortally wounded by him, takes the prize. It is the first visual presentation of a joke, already in use on the stage, which was to become a stock image of early cinema: the lover, minus his breeches, escaping through a window. It is a conceit which never fails to draw laughs. Hogarth manifestly enjoyed pioneering it, and Mack Sennett used it time and again in the silent days of Hollywood. Again, Laurel and Hardy, devoted students of Hogarth, took it up, and used it at least three times. In one version, the pair are in an empty street where Laurel, by mistake, fires a shot. At once, every upper window in the street opens, and scores of lovers, each trouserless, drop to the ground and run for it, each fearing the angry shotgun of an outraged husband. Here (one feels) Hogarth would have laughed to see his concept taken up with such energy.

Hogarth supplemented his series satires with a number of one-off subjects, some of superlative quality: *Strolling Actresses Dressing in a Barn*, *The Enraged Musician*, *The March to Finchley*, *The Cockpit* (or *Pit Ticket*), and *Southwark Fair*. The last contains twenty-two separate incidents and requires considerable information to be "read" properly. *Actresses* must have been done from life and is rich in sexuality and inside knowledge of the theater. The *Musician* illustrates eleven different kinds of annoying sounds. Indeed noise plays a leading part in many of Hogarth's concepts. The *March* illustrates the propensity of soldiers to beget illegitimate children, in itself tragic but cranked up by Hogarth's imagination into a boisterous comedy. All these works are chaos pictures, events getting out of control in a comic fashion: in *Southwark Fair*, a roof and scaffolding collapse, upending an actress and exposing her naked thighs, and in *The Cockpit* the crowd is chaotically insensate with greed and partisanship, a blind man in the middle being the only sign of calm; this too was done from life. Not all Hogarth's moral stories are of equal merit. *Industry and Idleness* and *The Four Stages of Cruelty*, though ingeniously conceived and powerful in conception, were engraved quickly and cheaply for a low-price popular market (no paintings) and lack sophistication.

On the other hand, Hogarth's satire on political elections, from major paintings done in the mid-1750s, represent the peak of his art. The satire was inspired by disgraceful doings in Oxford a year before, and Hogarth aimed to expose the full panoply of corruption whereby men got into the House of Commons, and parties, especially the Whigs, got into power. The first of these, *An Election Entertainment*, is Hogarthian comedy at its most direct, brutal, and bizarre. It involves nearly forty characters, and is painted with exceptional skill and daring. Most of the characters are drunk. One of the two candidates is embraced by a disgusting, gin-sodden old woman, while a drunken man empties the ashes of his pipe on his wig. The candidate's wife is sandwiched between two yokels, one of whom sings while holding his glass of wine over her head. The second candidate desperately tries to entertain three drunks by turning his hand into a baby's head (a trick Hogarth himself loved to perform). The mayor, fainting from a surfeit of oysters, has his head bathed, and one of the Whig street ruffians, hit on the head with a brick, has raw spirits poured into the wound by a fellow rough. Bricks, hurled by Tory opponents from the street outside, whizz through the open window, and one has just knocked over the party lawyer, who has been adding up the number of "certain" votes from a poll book. A clergyman takes off his wig to mop his bald head, while a bagpipe, violin, and bull fiddle sound off behind him. Drink is available, literally, in great tubs. Some of the faces are bestial in their vile distortions, and the noise, stench, belching, and cries of glee and derision are almost palpable. The candidates are part of the ruling class but, come election time, they are made to pay for it briefly by sucking up to the people in all their vulgar enormity—and that is what the painting is about. Here, indeed, is the putative democracy in which Britain, alone in the world, rejoiced, and Hogarth shows it in all its naked turpitude.

The final picture in the election series, *Chairing the Member*, shows the process complete. The Whigs have won, and one of them, now an MP, is being carried in triumph through the streets. But his posture is precarious, for his bearers are drunk, and a huge sow and her piglets have charged through their legs. The MP in fact is about to be precipitated into the stream which flows through the little town. Two partisans, an agricultural laborer with a flail and a one-legged sailor with a truncheon, fight it out in the foreground. To the left, Whig grandees feast their victory at the inn, while on the right a lady faints, while a little boy urinates onto the head of a monkey, itself on the shoulders of a dancing bear. The huge panorama of chaos, with about fifty figures, is composed with great art and terrific gusto—the central item of the chaired member introducing the new Hogarthian device of the tottering tower, about to collapse, a comic invention which was to appear again and again in British art, and is the acme and culmination of the chaotic spirit. In the bottom right-hand corner, a blind, bearded fiddler strums away at a postelection jig of joy—Hogarth never omits to put in the sound effects.

There is no doubt about the general success of Hogarth's work, based as it was on a combination of social satire, acute observation, and truthful comedy. He found England essentially a country without a school of art, dependent on imported masters. He left it with a distinctive tone of voice, all its own, preparing the way for Reynolds, Thomas Gainsborough, the Royal Academy, and the great school of watercolor painters. I am not saying that all were influenced by him, though many were. What *is* true, however, is that Hogarth gave the British artist self-confidence. He asserted, on every possible occasion, and in his writings, especially his major work, *The Analysis of Beauty*, and in his "Apology for Painters," which directly addresses the state of the arts in Britain, that his countrymen had the talent to produce the best, and had no need to bring foreign artists to London. He publicly attacked those, like William Kent (the interior designer and furniture maker), who took all their ideas (he said) from France and Italy. All British artists needed was a fair chance. Thus he published two pamphlets (around 1733) demanding copyright protection for engravers, designers, and etchers, and was the leading spirit in getting a protective statute through Parliament in 1735. This transformed the trade, led to a print shop opening at every street corner in fashionable London, and made the careers of Thomas Rowlandson, James Gillray, George Cruikshank, and countless others possible. He also admitted the need for systematic training, and set up an art school for that purpose. But he opposed the idea of what later became the Royal Academy, with its art school, all under royal patronage. He thought such patronage, as in France, would lead to artists kowtowing to the state and those who ruled it. He was indeed all for private enterprise, in the arts as in everything else, and could have given some points to Adam Smith, then a young man, for his future *Wealth of Nations*. He wanted the arts to flourish in a thoroughly English way: free, independent, nationalistic, and popular, but without being too democratic, for he was horribly aware, as his pictures show, how badly the common people could behave. He was inclined to be xenophobic. On his only trip abroad, he was arrested, as a spy, for drawing the fortifications of Calais. He responded with one of his best canvases, *O the Roast Beef of Old England* (or *The Gate of Calais*), showing himself at work, skeletal French soldiers, and a fat monk eagerly anticipating getting his hands on an imported side of prime English beef.

Hogarth was not only opposed to royal support of the arts, and its implicit control, but against patronage of any kind, if it could possibly be avoided. He wanted to hit hard, all the time, without any restraining aristocratic hand on his arm. So, while he joyfully accepted individual commissions, when he could get them, at a fair market price, he always dealt directly with the public, selling his prints himself to the shops, and organizing auctions for his paintings. These were often flops, for the public was not yet used to getting its fine art in such a fashion. Later in the century he could have got Christie's to help him— but they were sure to have quarreled. He had a tremendous temper, which Jane was not always able to mitigate. When in 1751 he auctioned the eight *Marriage à-la-mode* pictures, there was only one bidder, who got them cheap. Hogarth was so furious he smashed the gilded head of Van Dyck which was the sign of his business premises in Leicester Fields. Other auctions he organized fetched disappointing sums: *A Harlot's Progress* went for eighty-four guineas, *A Rake's Progress* for 176. *Strolling Actresses* was a snip at twenty-six guineas, and Horace Walpole bought the superb portrait of Sarah Malcolm for five guineas. On the other hand, Hogarth contrived to sell over one thousand copies of some of his engraving sets at a guinea each set, and this was a real profit, for he employed no middleman-publisher. When Simon Fraser, Lord Lovat, was about to be executed for his part in the Forty-Five Rebellion, Hogarth did a sketch of him from life, and the print he produced sold over five thousand copies at a shilling each. When he had a major public row with the demagogue John Wilkes, and his tame poet, Charles Churchill, Hogarth did a print of Wilkes which created his image for all time, and sold over seven thousand copies. One of Churchill as a bear, drinking a mug of ale, sold well too. Hogarth was never exactly rich, but he lived well and stayed out of debt. In addition to his house in what is now Leicester Square, in the heart of London, he acquired a country villa to the west, near what is now known as the Hogarth Roundabout. It is elegant, without being lavish, and has one fine projecting window, a joke in itself.

Some of Hogarth's paintings have been lost: the original of *Strolling Actresses*, for instance. But the prints, as Lamb recognized, form an art library in themselves. And the many surviving paintings are among the glories of the National Gallery, the National Portrait Gallery, and especially Sir John Soane's Museum in Lincoln's Inn Fields. Hogarth was always interesting—he never painted anything dull in his entire life—but at times he took a grand jump into the highest reaches of art, as with *The Graham Children*, a superb group portrait of three little girls, their brother, their cat, and their pet bird. Van Dyck, Velázquez, nor Goya could have produced a finer window into the lives of children, which has the added merit of humor, and the frisson caused by the attempts of the ferocious cat to get the little caged bird. But most of Hogarth's works are windows into life as it was lived in the eighteenth century. For instance, *Captain Lord George Graham in His Cabin* is the only detailed view we have of what the living quarters, aboard ship, of a senior naval officer looked like. We could be much better informed, of course, if all Hogarth's drawings and sketchbooks had survived, but few have. Early on he formed a habit of jotting down in pencil or ink anything interesting he saw. When he was still an apprentice-engraver, one of his mates recorded that, on a Sunday excursion to Highgate, they

witnessed a tavern brawl, one man hitting another on the head
with a tankard:

> The blood running down the man's face, together with
> the agony of the wound, which had distorted his features
> into the most hideous grin, presented Hogarth, who
> showed himself thus early "applied of the mode Nature
> had intended he should pursue," with too laughable a
> subject to be overlooked. He drew out his pencil and pro-
> duced on the spot one of the most ludicrous figures that
> ever was seen.

Hogarth called this sketching process "studying." He said
he liked thus to "collect" from London life. Of course he was
enormously inventive and imaginative. But I think it can truly
be said that none of the characters and incidents in his marvelous crowd scenes was without a foundation in truth, often an
event he had actually witnessed, and very likely recorded on
the spot. To Hogarth, life was in many ways a tragedy. The
example of his father showed it to be so, and in his own life
he had to take many hard knocks from fortune. But if existence was a tragedy at the core, it had an immense periphery
of comedy, with characters of every kind crowding in to make
us laugh and to enable us, as Dr. Johnson put it, "to enjoy life
or to endure it." No one in the history of art has set about
presenting this rich periphery so systematically and successfully. He is the supreme comic artist, and he will be raising
fascinated laughter in countless generations to come.

# CHAPTER TWO

# BENJAMIN FRANKLIN: FOUNDING FATHER OF AMERICAN LAUGHS

T HE LAST LETTER Hogarth received, the day before his death on 26 October 1764, was from Benjamin Franklin, ordering a complete set of his prints "for my publishing business in Philadelphia, and for my private enjoyment." So Franklin (1706–1790) knew what was good for him all right, and good for his customers. But then he knew, in terms of useful, practical knowledge, a great deal—more than his contemporaries, and as much as any man who ever lived. He was a commonsense polymath on a heroic scale. He had precisely the qualities that made, and have kept, America great. He has often been called "the First American," for during his lifetime the American character emerged with a flourish: as colonial Americans fought their way to independence, they drew up the first successful republican constitution, and put it to work in so thorough a manner that it has lasted to this day—suitably amended, of course. Franklin was the original can-do American, to whom nothing was impossible. He was also the first American humorist. He invented American humor, and many of its devices, including the one-liner. Moreover he invented the national mood in which American humor has flourished: that the world is a good and cheerful place, and everyone has an equal right to be happy in it. If you're not happy, Franklin argued, then very probably there is something the matter with *you*, not the world.

Certainly, Franklin at the end of his long life had every reason to consider that his life had been a happy one. His curriculum vitae is a marvel. His father made candles and soap in Boston, and Franklin left school at ten to assist him. That did not stop him from acquiring a vast amount of book-learning, as well as practical experience, and in due course he founded an academy that became one of America's finest colleges, the University of Pennsylvania. At twelve he was apprenticed to his half brother, a printer, and learned the trade from top to bottom. At seventeen he ran off to Philadelphia, and soon went to England to buy the latest equipment for a printing works of his own (he crossed the Atlantic eight times in his life—a record for a landlubber, I think). He made the *Pennsylvania Gazette* into one of the best and most successful newspapers of the day. He fathered two illegitimate children, and two lawful ones by his admirable wife, Deborah Read. He taught himself four languages. He became a power in Philadelphia intellectual circles, in its municipal politics, and then in national politics. He invented the lightning condenser, and his discoveries in electrostatics place him among the greatest American researchers in pure science. He served in the Pennsylvania assembly from 1751 to 1763, and was deputy postmaster general for all the thirteen colonies from 1753 until the Revolution. He strongly advocated federation and drew up the Albany Plan (1754), which adumbrated the U.S. Constitution. He acted as agent for Pennsylvania in London, got an honorary doctorate from Oxford, had another spell in London as agent for four states, and did everything in his considerable power to effect a peaceful settlement between Britain and the colonies. War being certain, he returned to America in 1775 to serve in the Second Continental Congress, and was a member of the committee which drew up the Declaration of Independence. In 1776 he was sent to France to get French help and persuaded France to recognize the new republic two years later. With John Adams and John Jay he negotiated the Treaty of Paris which ended the War of Independence in 1783. As a member of the Constitutional Convention in 1787 he was one of the signatories of the Constitution. He also wrote a superb autobiography and many other works.

Yet though his achievements were prodigious, he was not a prodigy in any offensive sense. He was, rather, the average man writ large, with huge energies, wide interests, powerful faculties, and purposeful tenacity of unusual strength. And he knew how to laugh, and to make others laugh. This propensity developed early. His half brother James, publisher and editor of the Boston paper *New England Courant*, which he had recently founded, was surprised and delighted to receive pseudony-mously, through the post, an article satirizing the local Calvin-ist bigwigs, especially Cotton Mather. The piece was signed Silence Dogood. The Boston religious establishment was then all-powerful and held to be above criticism. Miss Dogood's work was not only critical, it was savage—but also funny. James Franklin published it, and the response was gratifying—both noisily hostile, from the Calvinists, and quietly appreciative, from others. More pieces arrived, and more were published. In due course, it emerged that Silence Dogood was none other than James's sixteen-year-old apprentice and brother, Benja-min. These attacks on fashionable and well-entrenched Cal-vinist leaders, accusing them of moral and religious hypocrisy, reads well even today. At the time (1722) they aroused bitter resentment and made it difficult for young Franklin to make his way in the city—it was one reason he fled to Philadelphia, with its much more liberal intellectual climate. He continued to write, however, while learning the publishing trade and pre-paring to set up his own empire in print.

The whole business of religion nagged at him. Was there a God? And if so, what sort of God was He—and how should he cope with Him? In 1725, in London buying printing ma-chinery, he wrote a pamphlet from a Deist viewpoint, but pushing the concept to its logical limits. *A Dissertation on Lib-erty and Necessity, Pleasure and Pain*, composed when he was nineteen, argued powerfully that Deism led logically to the end of free will. If the universe was a piece of complex clockwork, mechanistically run by immutable natural laws, then there could be no freedom of will or ethical responsibility. So reason and virtue, however praised by the Deists themselves, were illusory. The argument was set down in a matter-of-fact manner, and not without humor, but the conclusions horrified the author, and he began to regret having written it as soon as it was published. Indeed he made efforts to recall and destroy all copies. Thus, in a sense, within three teenage years, Franklin had found wanting both the prevailing Calvinism of New England, and the cold, barren, and discouraging Deism which seemed the only alternative. Was there not a third choice—a system of religious belief and moral conduct more suited to the American character, with its optimism, doctrine of hard work and enjoyment, and confidence in the future?

Franklin was not an intellectual. That is, he did not believe ideas mattered more than people. Nor did he want to spend his life thinking and writing. He wanted to be up and doing, as businessman and local big shot, eventually as public benefactor. He needed to make money, to acquire a fortune sufficient to give him freedom of action. The printing concern he set up in Philadelphia was designed to achieve this aim. And in seeking to make it profitable he almost by accident hit on a scheme which also gave him a powerful way of making his voice heard: he went into the almanac trade. Between 1650 and 1750, in both Britain and America, almanacs made more money for publishers than any other product. As early as the 1660s, British sales of almanacs were close to half a million a year, and in America their sales, throughout the seventeenth and eighteenth centuries, outsold all other books combined. An almanac (the word is Arabic in origin) can be defined as a book of tables, produced annually, containing a calendar of months and days, with astronomical data and calculations, astrological forecasts, weather predictions, plus religious and secular anniversaries and much other useful information. They were common, in manuscript form, as early as the age of Roger Bacon and Chaucer, and as small printed books were universal in Shakespeare's day. They appealed to the simpleminded and were useful to the sophisticated, and when printing brought the price down radically, they were to be found in every literate household. Among other things, you could plan your travel and visits months ahead, for an almanac gave the moon phases accurately. As Shakespeare put it in *A Midsummer Night's Dream* (3.1):

Snout. Doth the Moone shine that night wee play our play?
Bottom. A Calender, a Calender! Looke in the Almanack, finde out the Moonshine!

By Franklin's time, the most successful publisher, Nathaniel Ames, sold up to sixty thousand copies a year of his *Astronomical Diary*. Franklin went into the trade in 1729, and three years later decided to produce a distinctive almanac of his own, following the precedent of Jonathan Swift who had written one twenty-three years before. For this purpose, he adopted the publishing pseudonym of "Richard Saunders, Polymath," and called the book *Poor Richard's Almanac*. It sold wholesale as well as retail, at three shillings and sixpence a dozen, for in a vast country like America where stationery shops were scarce, traders bought for resale, and Franklin often disposed of his stock in dozens, twenty-five dozens, even a thousand copies. He soon got up to ten thousand a year, and though he never outsold Ames, he cornered the educated market. Poor Richard always pleaded his poverty, and when his almanac took off, he announced in the 1734 edition that as a result he had been able to buy his wife "a pot and something to put into it, a pair of shoes, two new shifts and a new warm petticoat, and I have bought a second-hand new coat."

Poor Richard invited reader participation. He looked the reader in the eye, rather as Hogarth's lady did in the last plate of *A Harlot's Progress*. The motto was "share the joke," and there were plenty of jokes to share, for the essence of *Poor Richard's Almanac* was humor. Franklin sold in all thirteen colonies and his aim was to create, and then appeal to, all-American humor. There were plenty of blank spaces in almanacs, for the tables were of different sizes, and "the sayings of Poor Richard" served as fillers. The tone was smart aleck (a term Franklin may have invented), sometimes coarse, but also mixed with safe/proverbial, and always short and pithy. Thus:

Force shits upon reason's back.

Prithee, isn't Miss Coe's a comical case?
She lends out her tail and borrows her face.

Great talkers, little doers.

Gifts burst rocks.

Tell a miser he's rich, and a woman she's old,
　　You'll let no money of one, nor kindness of t'other.

Light purse, heavy heart.

Hunger never saw bad bread.

Marry your son when you will,
　　but your daughter when you can.

Industry need not wish.

The greatest monarch on the proudest horse is obliged
　　to sit upon his own arse.

One good husband is worth two good wives,
　　for the scarcer things are, the more they are valued.

When man and woman die, a poet sung,
　　His heart the last part moves, her last her tongue.

God heals, and the doctor takes the fees.

He's a fool that makes the doctor his heir.

God works wonders now and then.
　　Behold a lawyer—an honest man!

A countryman between two lawyers is like
　　a fish between two cats.

Never spare the parson's wine, nor the baker's pudding.

Eyes and priests bear no jests.

It can fairly be said that the one-liner, the quintessential form of American humor, was born in *Poor Richard's Almanac*—the short joke subsequently used by politicians from Henry Clay to Ronald Reagan, and by writers from Mark Twain to Dorothy Parker. Long after Franklin stopped publishing Poor Richard, he continued to manufacture one-liners, often by the midnight oil, sometimes on the spur of the moment. And many have stuck, and are found in the anthologies. In 1776, sweating out the Declaration of Independence, he said, "We must all hang together or, most assuredly, we shall all hang separately." He wrote in 1783 during the Treaty of Paris negotiations, "There never was a good war, or a bad peace." In his old age, in a letter to one of his French friends on 13 November 1789, he wrote, "Our constitution is in actual operation. Everything appears to promise that it will last. But in this world nothing is certain but death and taxes." "Remember," he laid down in *Advice to a Young Tradesman*, "that time is money." In *Thoughts on Commercial Subjects*, he coined the phrase "No nation was ever ruined by trade." Boswell also credits him with the axiom "Man is a tool-making animal." Franklin reflects many moods in his litany of one-liners, but the prevailing one is practical cynicism: "If you want to keep your secret from an enemy, tell it not to a friend."

Franklin worked hard all his long life, and played hard too. His broadmindedness on sexual matters was remarkable coming from a man born in Boston, raised in Calvinism, and prominent in public affairs for over half a century. Perhaps the most remarkable instance of it is a document headed "Advice to a Young Man on the Choice of a Mistress," in the form of a letter addressed to "My dear Friend," written in 1745 when Franklin was thirty-nine. It begins by praising marriage, which is presented as "right, pleasurable and of utility." But if a man is unable to marry, for one reason or another, and finds he cannot do without sex, then "in all your amours, you should *prefer old women to young ones.*" He then gives his reasons, addressing the problem in exactly the same practical spirit that he brought to designing a stove for a log cabin or a lightning-conductor for a church steeple.

He gives eight reasons for his advice. He never actually defines "old" and "young," though the inference is that by "young" he means sixteen to forty, and "old" is forty to sixty. His first reason is that an older woman knows more. So her "conversation is more improving, and more lastingly agreeable." Second, "When women cease to be handsome, they study to be good." There is thus an "augmentation of utility" in their behavior and they are capable of doing "a thousand services, small and great," especially if you are sick. Third, "there is no hazard of children" (here he speaks from experience, having begotten two bastards). Fourth, your affair with such a woman is unlikely to become public knowledge, since an older woman is "more prudent and discreet in conducting an intrigue to prevent suspicion." Any "commerce with them" is "safer" (perhaps an indirect reference to the diminished likelihood of contracting venereal disease, a matter on which Franklin was extremely careful throughout his life, unlike his younger contemporary Boswell). Fifthly, Franklin points out that it is essentially a woman's face and neck which grows old in such a way as to show it: "Below the girdle, it is impossible, of two women, to know an old from a young one." Moreover, "The pleasure of corporal enjoyment with an old woman is at least equal and frequently superior, every knack being by practice capable of improvement." Sixthly, "the sin is less." "Debauching a virgin" is bad; it is more pardonable to enjoy an experienced matron. Seventhly, there are your own feelings of guilt or satisfaction to consider. "The having made a young girl *miserable* may give you frequent bitter reflections, none of which can attend the making an old woman happy." Lastly, "They are so *grateful*."

This piece of intimate sociology, or perhaps better called psychology, would have been remarkable in any age. Its appearance in 1745, the year that Jonathan Edwards, the great preacher, was preparing his revivalist masterwork, *A Treatise Concerning the Religious Affections*, is astounding. It is true that in France, Crébillon fils published his daring work *La Sopha*, in which this piece of furniture recounts remarks of lovers who sat on it, but there was nothing remotely like it in the English-speaking world, and in the thirteen colonies, the Great Awakening was in progress, with campfire evangelism carrying all before it. Franklin originally, it seems, intended to publish his advice, rather like Lord Chesterfield in England. But he had second thoughts, and the document did not see the light for another two hundred years.

That Franklin enjoyed the favors of many women, young and old, American, English, and French, is a fact. But being an American, and a typical American, he upheld the primacy, if not exactly the sanctity, of marriage always, and his own was long-lasting and, so far as we can see, happy. He wrote to Mademoiselle Brillon, a Parisian salon owner, that promiscuity, within reason, was permissible, and compared it to a lady expertly playing an instrument and numerous men enjoying the music. But he also insisted that "two heads are better than one in weighty matters" and that marriage proved it. And he wrote to his wife, whom he called "Debbie," after a dozen years of matrimony,

> Of the Chloës and Phyllises poets may prate.
> I sing my plain country Joan.
> Now twelve years my wife, still the joy of my life,
> Blest day that I made her my own.

In short Franklin was a case of an American hedonist getting it both ways, and preaching, evenhandedly, domestic bliss and sexual adventurism. Moreover the thing is always done in a jovial spirit and with full regard for all the practical mishaps which may attend departure from the straight and narrow. Franklin was commenting on John Locke's famous dictum in his *The Reasonableness of Christianity*, published a generation earlier, that "today, virtue is by far the best bargain," by saying, "As a general rule, undoubtedly Yes! But there may be exceptions, for the prudent and circumspect."

America has always been a lucky country. In addition to a most extensive, varied, rich, highly exploitable, and beautiful real estate, America possessed, in her Founding Fathers, one of the most talented groups of men ever brought together for a public purpose. Among them, Benjamin Franklin was eminent; some would say, with the possible exception of Washington himself, preeminent. He gave to the foundational mixture a rare genius for humor, which has become part of the national character, and gives it a wonderful savor.

Franklin was always precocious, and at the age of twenty-two he composed his own epitaph:

The Body of
B. Franklin,
Printer;
Like the Cover of an old Book,
Its contents torn out,
And stript of its Lettering and Gilding,
Lie here, Food for Worms.
But the work shall not be wholly lost,
For it will, as he believed, appear once more,
In a new & more perfect Edition,
Corrected and Amended
By the Author.

A good joke. An even better one is that the actual headstone reads simply "Benjamin and Deborah Franklin 1790." All that is needed.

# CHAPTER THREE

# DR. JOHNSON: MELANCHOLY MERRIMENT

I T STRETCHES CREDULITY to write of Dr. Samuel Johnson (1709–1784) as a comic. Most people would think of him as the antithesis: solemn, even sententious, severe, judgmental, strongly opposed to frivolity in manners, censoring jokes on a wide range of subjects—religion, the clergy, especially bishops, sinfulness, and, above all, death. There were four reasons why, on the face of it, comedy had little part in his life. First, he was by nature somber, suffering throughout his life from what he called "a vile melancholy." Second, his health was poor for, though he was immensely strong and lived to the age of seventy-five with his chief faculties intact, he was a victim of numerous ailments, causing at times pain, distress, and even incapacity, spasms, twinges, aches, and convulsions, daily reminders of mortality. Third, he was painfully aware both of his capacities and of the psychological weaknesses which prevented him from making full use of them. To him, this was sinful, and he saw his life as a permanent sin. Diary entries and prayers, especially on great feasts of the church when he reviewed his life (and his birthdays), show his despair at curbing his faults and doing energetically what he ought to do. His actual achievements he saw as minor, and he was forever conscious of remissness, perpetual sloth, and failure. Finally, he had a fear of death which amounted to an obsession, and a terror of hell at times amounting almost to mania. There were dark and deep corners in his personality he dreaded to explore.

Yet the fact remains that Dr. Johnson contrived to get an enormous amount of fun out of life, and to provide fun for a vast range of other people. They crowded around him to hear what he had to say; primarily, no doubt, to gather wisdom and guidance but also in the comfortable knowledge that he would give them cause to laugh periodically. The eager silences in which he held forth to all-attentive listeners were punctuated by great shouts and barrages of laughter. There is endless testimony to the power, frequency, volume, and infectiousness of his laughter. He would often say, Mrs. Thrale records, "that the size of a man's Understanding might always be known by his Mirth." She adds,

His own was never contemptible. He would laugh at a stroke of Absurdity, or a Saillie of genuine Humour more heartily than I almost ever saw a man, and though the Jest was often such as few felt besides himself, yet his Laugh was irresistible, & was observed immediately to produce that of the Company, not merely from the notion that it was proper to laugh when he did, but purely for want of Power to forbear it.

Johnson himself, though freely admitting his melancholy, also boasted of his humor. In 1775, James Boswell (his well-known biographer) records him saying, "It is wonderful, Sir, how rare a quality good humour is in life. We meet with very few good-humoured men." Boswell mentioned Sir Joshua Reynolds, Edmund Burke, Bennet Langton, and Topham Beauclerk (all founding members of Johnson's Literary Club), "but none of whom he would allow to be good humoured." Langton was "muddy," Beauclerk was "acid," and so on. "Then, shaking his head and stretching himself at his ease in the coach, and smiling with much complacency, he turned to me and said: 'I look upon *myself* as a good-humoured fellow.'" But this Boswell would not allow.

No, no, Sir, that will not do. You are good natured, but not good humoured. You are irascible. You have not patience with folly and absurdity. I believe you would pardon them, if there were time to deprecate your vengeance: but punishment follows so quick after sentence, that they cannot escape.

Johnson, however, defended his good humor. And indeed, Boswell, like Mrs. Thrale, gives many instances of it: Sir John Hawkins, a rather dour person himself ("an unclubbable man," as Johnson put it), who nonetheless wrote a good and useful *Life* of Johnson, insisted, "In the talent of humour there hardly ever was his equal." Hawkins thought that only Shakespeare's Tarlton was his equal. Hawkins wrote, "Gesticular, mimicry, and buffoonery he hated, and would often huff Garrick for exercising it in his presence, but of the talent humour he had an almost enviable portion." Hawkins says, "it was ever of that arch and dry kind, which lies concealed under the appearance of gravity." He had a talent for imitative satire, making fun of the more pretentious style of essay writing. As an instance, Hawkins quotes his "meditation on a pudding," which is not found in his *Complete Works*, but was evidently given on various occasions, once during his tour of the Hebrides.

Indeed it is likely that Johnson's greatest explosions of fun went unrecorded, for explosions they were, difficult to put down in words, or even to remember the gist of them. They occurred quite spontaneously, when something struck Johnson as irresistibly funny. Then he would go on fantasizing and laughing, until exhausted. All really funny talkers have this gift: Sydney Smith particularly, Oscar Wilde, G. K. Chesterton. Mark Twain had it too and Alexander Woollcott. Stephen Spender and Barbara Skelton insisted Cyril Connolly had it, on rare occasions, when the word for it was "magnificent," but I only heard faint echoes of this gigantic gift. Sir Isaiah Berlin had it, and I heard him: but the trouble was, once he got really going on a line of fantastic humor, he began to speak so fast, and his accent became so impenetrable, that the sense was

difficult to grasp, though his evident delight in his fun was so
furious that you laughed all the same.

That Johnson had this gift, which amounts to a kind of
genius, is clear, for Boswell was able to reconstruct one instance
of it, at least in part. It took place in the room of Sir Robert
Chambers, the eminent lawyer, in the Temple. Chambers said
he had that day drawn up Bennet Langton's will. Langton had
no son but three sisters, whom Johnson always referred to, un-
kindly, as "the three *Dowdies.*" Langton was determined they
should get his property instead of his nearest male cousin, and
the will made this certain. So, said Chambers, Langton was
very pleased with himself and the day's proceedings. The incident suddenly struck Johnson as hilarious:

*He now laughed immoderately, without any reason that we
could perceive*, at our friend's making his will. He called
him "the testator," and added: "I daresay he thinks he
has done a mighty thing. He won't stay till he gets home
to his seat in the country. . . . He'll call up the landlord
of the first inn on the road; and, *after a suitable preface
upon mortality and the uncertainty of life*, will tell him
that he should not delay making his will; and here, Sir,
will he say, is *my* will, which I have just made, with the
assistance of one of the ablest lawyers in the kingdom
(*laughing all the time*). He believes he has made his will,
but he did not make it. You, Chambers, made it for him.
I trust you have more conscience than to make him say

"being of sound understanding"—Ha, ha, ha!—*I'd have his will turned into verse, like a ballad.*

Embarrassed, Chambers was glad when they left his room. He did not get the joke, wills being "mighty serious things" for lawyers. But "Johnson could not stop his merriment and continued it all the way till we got without the Temple-gate. He then burst into such a fit of *laughter, that he appeared to be almost in a convulsion* and in order to support himself, laid hold of one of the posts." Boswell concludes that he "sent forth peals so loud, that in the silence of the night his voice seemed to resound from Temple-bar to Fleet-ditch."

There was another occasion of Johnsonian hilarity, occasioned by one of his comic fantasies, recorded by Fanny Burney (later Fanny Burney D'Arblay, the novelist and diarist). Staying the weekend at the Thrales' house at Streatham, she was astonished to find that Johnson, "this great and dreaded lord of English literature," could display "a turn for burlesque humour." Next morning at breakfast, the talk again flowed "copiously," with Johnson urging her to write a comedy for the stage. Suddenly, she and Mrs. Thrale noticed

that Johnson, see-sawing in his chair, began laughing to himself so heartily as to almost shake his seat as well as his sides. We stopped . . . hoping he would reveal the subject of his mirth, but he enjoyed it inwardly, without heeding our curiosity—till at last he said he had been struck with a notion that Miss Burney "would begin her dramatic career by writing a piece called *Streatham*." He paused, and laughed yet more cordially, and then suddenly commanded a pomposity to his countenance and his voice, and added: "Yes! *Streatham—a Farce!*"

It is true that Johnson cannot with any regard to truth be called a comic writer. There are jokes in *The Idler* and *The Rambler*, but they are like plover's nests or the quotations from Horace in Mr. Gladstone's speeches—you have to be shown them. On the other hand, his talk abounded with humor, whether he was being didactic, argumentative, abusive, censorious, singing praises, or calling down the wrath of the gods. And the humor too was of many kinds: verbal wit, gentle pleasantry, outrageous buffoonery, or sheer abuse.

The sayings of Dr. Johnson, which are memorable or at any rate remembered, amount to at least a thousand by my reckoning. The *Oxford Dictionary of Quotations* lists 276, which puts him fourth after Shakespeare, Alexander Pope, and Kipling. In a useful compilation of *Sayings of Doctor Johnson*, by Brenda O'Casey (for Duckworth), there are 768. They raise the question: What is comic, or what is humor? For many have no apparent power to make us laugh. But almost all make us hug ourselves with pleasure: we are glad they were spoken, and jotted down. For neatness, profundity, or aptness, pith, and force, they are an unrivaled collection. They make the *Pensées* of Pascal, or the sayings of Montesquieu or Cardinal de Retz, Montaigne, Madame du Deffand, Nicholas Chamfort, or Voltaire, seem by comparison meager.

Some of the best make you think: Is this true? And after
thinking about them you conclude that, true or not, you are
glad they were said. Thus: "Patriotism is the last refuge of a
scoundrel." "A man will turn over half a library to make one
book." "No man but a blockhead ever wrote but for money."
"In lapidary inscriptions a man is not upon oath." "Every man
has a right to utter what he thinks truth, and every other
man has a right to knock him down for it. Martyrdom is the
test." "When a man is tired of London, he is tired of life." "The
chief glory of every people arises from its authors." "Nothing
is more hopeless than a scheme of merriment." "When a man
knows he is to be hanged in a fortnight, it concentrates his
mind wonderfully." "There is now less flogging in our great
schools than formerly, but then less is learned there. So what
the boys get at one end, they lose at the other." "We would all
be idle if we could." "I wonder that women are not all Papists."
"Sir, the insolence of wealth will creep out." And in this group
there is an obscure and delightful remark I love to quote: "Sir,
among the anfractuosities of the human mind, I know not if it
may be one, that there is a superstitious reluctance to sit for a
picture." There are few people, perhaps none besides Johnson,
who can work a word like "anfractuosity" into a speech at a
convivial gathering. What does it mean? Why, tortuous.

Many of Johnson's sayings are harsh criticisms or sheer
abuse. If we delight in them, it is because we are not their
object; or because the person deserved it; or just for the joy of
hearing a harsh thing said neatly or elegantly or with punch,
or with inventive malice. He was asked to give an example

of "coarse raillery" among Thames boatmen, and produced:
"Sir, your wife, under pretence of keeping a bawdy-house,
is a receiver of stolen goods." To a man of limited intellect
in a tavern: "Sir, I have found you an argument, but I am
not obliged to find you an understanding." Of Bet Flint, a
Hogarthian woman known in Fleet Street: "She was generally
slut and drunkard—occasionally whore and thief." Of the
politician Dudley Long North he said: "He fills a chair." Of
Prime Minister Shelburne: "A mind as narrow as the neck of
a vinegar cruet." There were certain people—writers, public
performers, what we would call celebrities—who attracted
his arrows. Of the actor and playwright Samuel Foote: "Foote is
quite impartial. He tells lies of everybody." The actor Thomas
Sheridan he dismissed thus: "Such an excess of stupidity, Sir,
is not in nature." He had a word to say in praise of Thomas
Gray's *Elegy*, but of the poet himself he remarked, "Sir, he
was dull in company, dull in his closet, dull everywhere. He was
dull in a new way, and that made many people think him
*great*." Two other poets who attracted his censure were Samuel
Derrick and Christopher Smart. Asked which was the better,
he answered, "Sir, there is no settling the point of precedency
between a louse and a flea." After abusing Rousseau, "a very
bad man. I would sooner sign a sentence for his transportation
than that of any felon who has gone from the Old Bailey these
many years," he was asked if he was worse than Voltaire, and
replied, "Why, Sir, it is difficult to settle the proportion of
iniquity between them."

Two men, for personal reasons, drew down his wrath in

prodigious quantities. One was Lord Chesterfield, who promised help and patronage when Johnson began his dictionary, but in practice did nothing. Johnson joked, "This man I thought had been a Lord among wits, but I find he is only a wit among Lords." He castigated his famous *Letters* to his son, teaching behavior in society, summing the work up thus: "They teach the morals of a whore, and the manners of a dancing-master." When his *Dictionary* appeared, and Chesterfield sought to share the credit for it, Johnson wrote him a public letter of reproach, one of the finest letters ever written, denouncing the whole system of literary patronage as practiced in the eighteenth century: "Is not a Patron, my Lord, one who looks with unconcern on a man struggling for life in the water and, when he has reached ground, encumbers him with help?"

He had even harsher things to say about, and to, James Macpherson, who claimed credit for Ossian and was exposed by Johnson as a fraud. When Macpherson threatened violence, Johnson responded, "I will not desist from detecting what I think a cheat from any fear of the menaces of a ruffian." And he had another word to say on the wretched man's ideas of morals: "If he does really think that there is no distinction between virtue and vice, why, Sir, when he leaves our houses let us count our Spoons."

Did Dr. Johnson have it in for the Scots? It seems so, both as individuals and in general. He had a flaming row with Adam Smith, and he repeatedly attacked David Hume as an atheist: "I do not know indeed whether he has first been a blockhead and that has made him a rogue, or first been a rogue and that has made him a blockhead." He wrote fairly of Scotland when he went there, and thanks to Boswell made some good Scotch friends. But he could rarely resist a dig. "Mr. Ogilvie observed, that Scotland had a great many noble wild prospects. Johnson: 'I believe, Sir, you have a great many. Norway too has noble wild prospects; and Lapland is remarkable for prodigious noble wild prospects. But, Sir, let me tell you, the noblest prospects which a Scotchman ever sees, is the high road that leads him to England!'" This is a typical Johnsonian sally, making expert use of repetition and rising to a crescendo. But he was equally effective in his short, pithy remarks, notably on the Irish. Of their prodigious noble wild prospect, the Giant's Causeway, asked if it were worth seeing, he said: "Worth seeing? Yes. But not worth going to see." And: "The Irish are a *fair people*. They *never* speak well of one another." He went for the French too: "The French are a gross, ill-bred, untaught people. A lady there will spit on the floor and rub it with her foot." And: "A Frenchman must always be talking, whether he knows anything of the matter or not. An Englishman is content to say nothing, when he has nothing to say." As for Americans, he asked, "How is it we hear the loudest *yelps* for liberty among the drivers of negroes?" He said, "I am willing to love all mankind, *except an American*."

There were times when Dr. Johnson appeared to be critical of women, at least outside their sphere: "Sir, a woman's preaching is like a dog's walking on his hind legs. It is not done well. But you are surprised to find it done at all." And on the subject of legal arrangements: "Nature has given women

so much power that the law has very wisely given them little."
But Johnson liked female company, more so in many ways
than men's. "If I had no duties, and no reference to futurity,
I would spend my life in driving briskly in a post-chaise with
a pretty woman." He clearly liked sex. He told David Garrick, "I'll come no more [backstage at your theatre], David, for
the silk stockings and white bosoms of your actresses excite
my amorous propensities." This is Boswell's decorous way of
putting it. John Wilkes said the actual words used were "do
make my genitals to quiver." But if easily aroused, Johnson
believed ideas were at the heart of physical sex: "Were it not
for imagination, Sir, a man would be as happy in the arms of a
chambermaid as of a Duchess."

We know a lot about his preferences in women. He liked
a firm mind: "Poll [Carmichael] is a stupid slut. I had some
hopes of her at first, but when I talked to her tightly and
closely, I could make nothing of her. She was wiggle-waggle
and I could never persuade her to be categorical." He liked
them spotless: "I have often thought that if I kept a seraglio,
the ladies should all wear linen gowns, or cotton. I mean
stuffs made of vegetables substances. I would have no silk; you
cannot tell when it is clean." He believed in marriage, and
thought a man should marry "first, for virtue; secondly, for
wit; thirdly, for beauty; and fourthly, for money." He thought
bachelors aged badly: "They that have grown old in a single
state are generally found to be morose, fretful and captious." It
is true "marriage has many pains," but "celibacy has no pleasures." On the other hand a second marriage was a risk, "the

triumph of hope over experience." In choosing a wife, a man was not a good judge. When Boswell asked, "Do you not suppose that there are fifty women in the world, with any one of whom a man may be as happy as with any one woman in particular?" Johnson replied, "Ay, Sir, fifty thousand." He said, "Marriages would be as happy, and often more so, if they were all made by the Lord Chancellor." Yet he did not dispute that marriage was difficult: "Sir, it is so far from being natural for a man and woman to live in a state of marriage, that we find all the motives which they have for remaining in that connection, and the restraints which civilised society imposes to prevent separation, are hardly sufficient to keep them together."

But if Johnson viewed marriage with some misgivings, he spoke out unreservedly on behalf of friendship. "There is in this world no real delight (excepting those of sensuality) but exchange of ideas in conversation." And "the happiest conversation [is] where there is no competition, no vanity, but a calm quiet interchange of sentiments." Friendship arose "when you come close to a man in conversation." That took time. "John Wesley's conversation is good, but he is never at leisure. He is always obliged to go at a certain hour. This is very disagreeable to a man who loves to fold his legs and have out his talk, as I do." Moreover, the cult of friendship in conversation demands vivacity, which "is much an art, and depends greatly on habit." So: "I hate a fellow whom pride, or cowardice, or laziness drives into a corner, and [who] does nothing when he is there but sit and growl. Let him come out as I do, and *bark*." Friends were a "necessity of life." "Sir, I look upon every day to be lost, in which I do not make a new acquaintance." For "acquaintance may broaden into friendship." "If a man does not make new acquaintance as he advances through life, he will soon find himself left alone. A man, Sir, should keep his friendship in *constant repair.*"

So death was the enemy, of friendship as of anything else. When Boswell asked, "But is not the fear of death natural to man?" Johnson replied, "So much so, Sir, that the whole of life is but keeping away the thoughts of it." He laid down: "To neglect at any time preparation for death is to sleep on our post at a siege. But to omit it in old age is to sleep at an attack." In the year of his death, he said, "I struggle hard for life. I take physic, and take air. My friend's chariot is always ready. We have run this morning twenty-four miles, and could run forty-eight more. *But who can run the race with death?*" Friends were very loyal to him in his last weeks. But he wondered, "I know not whether I should wish to have a friend by me, or have it all between God and myself." His last words were "*iam moriturus*"—now I am about to die. The pithy phrase was with this "good-humoured man" till the last, and since then, as at the time, his sayings have been preserved and repeated, and have conveyed much excellent senses, and made us laugh, outwardly and, perhaps more important, inwardly.

# THOMAS ROWLANDSON: BOTTOMS UP!

T HOMAS ROWLANDSON (1756–1827) was in my view England's most perfect artist, doing what he chose to do better than anyone else. He was also a humorist whose jokes, vulgar though many of them are, never tire. I would rather live among a collection of Rowlandson's watercolor drawings than that of any other artist, just as Charles Lamb lived among Hogarth's. This is an idiosyncratic judgment. But then drawing is a peculiar and personal art, and when it has the object of raising laughter and spirits, individual taste takes precedence over any other factor.

Rowlandson was born into the London middle class, and counted himself a gentleman. His father, a wool and silk merchant, went bankrupt when Thomas was three, and he was brought up by a wealthy aunt in Soho, attending a good school and the Royal Academy Schools from the age of fourteen, and exhibiting his first watercolor at the academy when eighteen. It had the intriguing title of *Delilah Paying Samson a Visit while in Prison* but, alas, has disappeared. He spent some time in Paris, learning a lot, and drawing a superb comic scene of the Place des Victoires, as well as gathering material for two first-class pairs of drawings, contrasting British and French officers in their quarters, and the two armies in their camps at a review.

Rowlandson had a rich banker friend, Mathew Michell, owner of a Cornish estate. The rustic landscapes and drawings of villagers which he made on visits there form a superb group, similar to and on occasions better than Gainsborough's work in pencil and watercolor. Rowlandson was always hard-working. He learned engraving and turned many of his watercolors into prints. He had various well-born patrons, including the Prince of Wales, who bought his *Review* pair. All this was the respectable side. However, he also had a taste for low life, which he sampled in company with the gifted rural artist George Morland. Their relationship is immortalized in a wonderful watercolor, *A Brace of Blackguards*, showing Morland seated with a cudgel and Rowlandson standing by him in a boxing posture. Morland's weakness was drink, which ruined and killed him. Rowlandson's was gambling. He acquired this gentlemanly taste early on, and after his aunt died in 1789 and left him a substantial legacy, he became a high roller. It took him four years to get through the money but by 1793 he was on his uppers. He was forced to take on any work he could get, and it is from this period I date some of his pornographic drawings (again with the Prince of Wales as a secret patron). In 1797, however, Rudolph Ackermann opened his print shop in the Strand. Thereafter, for over twenty years, Rowlandson was one of his principal suppliers of watercolor drawings for prints. Since Ackermann was a first-class businessman, insisting on the highest standards, the partnership flourished. Rowlandson did individual pictures, illustrations for classic novels and new topographical works, such as the *Three Tours of Doctor Syntax*, and special series, such as *The Microcosm of London*, for which the elder Augustus Pugin did architectural settings. If Rowlandson wanted to turn out vulgar or pornographic material for quick, ready cash, he used Thomas Tegg of Cheapside (and possibly others). Thus, by industry and ingenuity, he made a good living and survived his occasional gambling spasms. But his health gave way in 1825 and he died two years later.

We know that Rowlandson was tall, burly, and good-looking, for he drew himself carefully on several occasions, and these portraits are confirmed by the work of other artists. He was a popular and decent man with a strong sense of honor. His output, which was prodigious, can be divided into four categories. First came the rustic drawings, not primarily humorous, done principally for Michell, who possessed 550 of them when he died in 1819. Next came the pornography. This was extensive and has never been professionally cataloged, though some of it has often been reproduced in furtive publications. With one or two exceptions it is not his best work. But it is immeasurably superior to most pornographic art. The titles tell their own tales: *The Toss Off, The Sanctified Sinner, The Modern*

*Pygmalion* (artists painting a naked model), *Fumble-Cunt, The Unexpected Visit, The Concert* (naked girls playing instruments to please an enthusiast), *The Miser* (another enthusiast clinging on to his money-box while enjoying sex), *The Curious Parson, Susannah and the Elders, The Happy Parson, The Tambourine, The Harem, The Pasha, Catherine the Great, The Swings,* and *The Intruder in the Convent.* In only a few cases does the original watercolor drawing, on which the print was based, survive, and the engravings are normally of poor quality. Despite this, Rowlandson put a good deal of his habitual energy and inventiveness into this hackwork. His habitual dislike of clergymen, Oxbridge dons, and stingy rich men comes out strongly, and his young women, showing their private parts with gusto and enjoyment, are often beautifully drawn. As always with Rowlandson, the composition brilliantly tells its story.

The third group, of highly finished pen and watercolor wash drawings, show Rowlandson at his best, and when in a good state of preservation, and carefully examined, reveal him as a great master. He had three outstanding gifts. First, he could arrange his figures in exactly the way he wanted to make his point with great clarity and force. Second, his figure drawing was superb: elegant, flowing, and wonderfully funny, if required. Third, he could lay on a wash more skillfully than any other English watercolorist whatsoever, so that the drawings glow. He mixed his washes with fiendish cunning to produce miraculous shades of dun and darkness, and the highlights sparkle in a way only the great Richard Bonington ever equaled. This top group encompasses a score of drawings.

One shows the famous Georgiana Cavendish, the Duchess of Devonshire, gambling with her sister, and others. There is a second gambling scene, all male (except for the buxom barmaid chalking up the drink score) and including Rowlandson himself, helping to part an inexperienced country bumpkin from his cash. The characters and facial expressions in these two drawings are wonderfully conveyed, and beneath the surface humor there is an almost photographic realism: greed, fear, hesitation, lust, bestial envy, and passionate avarice are all powerfully expressed. One can almost smell the sweat of obsession, even on the well-born women, and hear the rattle and fall of the dice, and the rustle of hands extracting golden guineas from velvet purses and reticules. These are two of the best drawings ever done in England (the first is in the Metropolitan Museum of Art, the second at Yale).

There are two more first-class drawings of Georgiana and her sister: one listening to a guitarist, the other at Covent Garden. The second is complemented by a highly detailed drawing done in the foyer, showing operagoers, including well-known figures, inspecting one another with critical eyes. These works convey superbly the elegant sharpness of upper-class life in the 1790s. Indeed, *Box Lobby Loungers*, as the latter is called, is drawn with infinite precision and skill and conveys a vast amount of information. Two more beautiful drawings, *Entrance to the Mall* and *Hyde Park Corner*, show high society tumultuously mixing with the hoi polloi. There is also a famous vignette of Dr. Johnson eating his dinner, with relish, in a booth. The skill with which this complex drawing is organized is prodigious—no other artist then living, British or French, could have managed it. One can spend an hour studying its details.

However, the undoubted masterpiece in this group, and the best thing Rowlandson ever did, is *Skaters on the Serpentine*, now in the National Museum of Wales, Cardiff. Apart from the fact that it is in a perfect state of preservation, so that the infinitely delicate color washes can be seen in their pristine freshness, the figure drawing is particularly agile and inventive. The comedy is delicious but is overshadowed by the sheer beauty of the scene—no one wishing to study how bare winter trees should be drawn and colored should neglect this work.

I have listed the greatest in this select group. But there are some favorites of mine I wish to add because they open windows into life, Rowlandson having a piercing eye for detail and acute accuracy in reproducing it. Thus *A Coach Booking Office* shows with almost photographic realism what one looked like, early in the morning, with the added interest of showing Rowlandson himself, and his friend Henry Wigstead, setting out on a journey. *The Band* portrays a four-man military combination at full blast, so that you can almost hear the beat and the row. *The Chambermaid* is a brilliant drawing of a fat, rich, and half-naked man in an inn bed trying to rape a pretty hotel servant who is trying to operate a bed warmer. *Henry Angelo's Fencing Academy*, done with enviable pen work and first-class color washing, depicts a famous institute of the late 1780s. The information conveyed in all these drawings is invaluable to historians of the age. But what also strikes me is their lively humanity. The sixteen people in the last are all wonderfully real, and recognizable to contemporaries. The kind of skill needed to compose such a complex drawing is rare indeed.

The fourth and last group comprises the rest of Rowlandson's work, comprising hundreds of drawings, many of which only survive in their engraved versions. In 1880 a connoisseur named Joseph Grego published a two-volume work, *Rowlandson the Caricaturist*, in which a very large number are listed, dated, and annotated. This rare work has been reproduced in facsimile by the American Collectors' Editions Ltd. but is still hard to get. Many of the prints were, and are, of poor quality. But it serves to indicate the range, scope, and volume of Rowlandson's output. What is really required is for Yale University Press, the leading publisher of catalogues raisonnés, to produce a complete volume of his works. This would be immensely difficult, for many of the original watercolor drawings, when they have not been lost completely, are in private hands, often unknown ones. But if accomplished, such a book would convey, for the first time, the true quality of his art, instead of the distorted and degraded versions produced by poor-quality commercial engravings.

Still, the splendid vigor and inventiveness of Rowlandson the humorist often emerges from the prints. There are two important points to be made. First, the essence of his humor was the accident. He was especially interested in the accident about to happen, or in the process of happening. He was a chaos-joker. What he really liked to do was to take as his starting point the "tottering tower" or "falling pyramid" image, first set up by Hogarth in his *Chairing the Member*, the last of his election series. Rowlandson turned this tottering moment into his essential comic art. In *The Hunt Supper*, the drunken squire, who has jumped on the table to roar out the hunting song more outrageously, is about to fall off, and join some of his fellow riders who are already sprawled on the floor. In *Winding the Clock*, the old gentleman who has climbed on a furniture pyramid to put the clock right is about to come crashing down. There are numerous drawings of riders colliding or about to fall off their horses, a subject which fascinated him. Or coaches and carriages in the process of toppling over. In *The Disaster*, a series of calamities are overwhelming a gouty man in his armchair because the lascivious housemaid, whose breasts are being fumbled by a blackamoor servant, has dropped her tea tray and knocked over a table.

These upsets are supplemented by what I call fight-about-to-break-out scenes. In *A Bull Bitch*, a terrified gentleman is about to have his face smashed in by the huge fist of a powerful woman, whose pretty young confederate has already stolen his watch and is about to stuff it into the cleavage of her exposed breasts. In *The White Sargent*, a furious young wife in her nightgown, with her breasts hanging out, is upbraiding her old hunting husband who is ensconced before a roaring fire with his glass of grog: "Why don't you come to bed, you drunken sot?" The white sargent (the angry wife in nightdress attacking an intoxicated husband returning late) is a constant figure in Rowlandson's repertoire of marital rows. There is another splendid fight about to break out between a furious butcher

and a young harridan with exposed breasts, in *The Quarrel*.
Her old hag confederate is pouring out a noggin of gin to give
her courage, though she doesn't look as though she needs it.
Rowlandson, like Dickens, was always ready to inflame his
disaster drawings with alcohol. He particularly liked to portray
women drinking. Thus *The Morning Dram* shows a society
lady having her hair dressed and about to consume a strong
glass of brandy, poured out for her by her tire-woman. But he
also loved drunken coachmen because they were the prime
cause of overthrown carriages, the source of so many of his
tottering fantasies.

Quite apart from his pornography, Rowlandson always
liked to bring sex into his drawings if he could with some
pretense of verisimilitude. Even more than exposed breasts,
he loved exposing women's bottoms. This was made possible
surprisingly often, to our view, by the nature of women's un-
derpinnings in the late eighteenth and early nineteenth centuries. Between 1785, when he first began drawing for the
market, and about 1825, ladies and respectable women never
wore what we would call panties, or knickers. They had in-
numerable petticoats beneath their skirts—half a dozen, even
ten, were customary. But the only women who habitually wore
drawers, as they were called, were those who needed to expose
their legs: actresses, especially dancers, to secure freedom of
movement, and prostitutes, who hitched up their skirts at
street corners to attract customers. These women had to have
drawers to avoid exposure of their private parts and pubic hair
in public places, which in some countries such as France and

Italy was a criminal offense. The Duke of Wellington used to tell the story that when Bonaparte returned to Paris at the end of 1812 after losing his entire army in Russia, he was anxious to distract the frivolous Parisians from his defeat by providing them with a talking point. So he ordered the dancers at the Paris Opera to discard their drawers. "But," said the duke, "the dancers, to their credit, flatly refused."

On the respectable side of the underclothes equation, women were not supposed to reveal their ankles, let alone anything above. They wore stockings, of course, but these usually came only up to just below the knee, or for evening attire just above it. One of Rowlandson's drawings, *Taking a Mean Advantage*, shows an unmannerly young fellow turning back to look at a young woman who is climbing a gate, thereby exposing a large expanse of naked thigh. It was an adage, dating from those times, that a gentleman always allowed a lady to go first, except when approaching a stile, when he preceded her to save her embarrassment. Much worse, however, were situations in which a woman's petticoats were not merely hitched up but fell over her head when she was turned upside down, thus exposing her pubic hair, pudenda, her thighs, and above all, her entire bottom.

Rowlandson, who like many humorists regarded bottoms (especially those of ladies) as an unending source of merriment, thus formulated joke devices which would enable him, plausibly and legitimately, to show ladies' bottoms as often as possible. I call it his "bottoms up" strategy, and he deployed it with endless resourcefulness and great success. It involved devising accidents which turned ladies upside down, and thus put their petticoats over their heads. A typical example is *Escape from a Fire*, in which a lady, trying to save some of her more precious household ornaments, has lifted up her nightdress to hold them, thus exposing her entire body up to the waist, to the delight of the firemen. In another brilliant drawing, *The Overturned Coach*, the vehicle has come to grief in the middle of a river, precipitating all its occupants into the water. In this ingenious drawing, three of the young women in the coach have been upended, exposing all their legs and bottoms. In *Taking a Five-barred Gate—Flying*, he shows a young lady, riding sidesaddle, whose horse has refused a gate, and sent her flying over it, her skirt and petticoats right up around her waist, and her legs and bottom exposed. While stretching the point a bit, this is a masterly piece of draftsmanship. I have counted thirty-five drawings in which the strategy is employed in various "accidents," and bottoms bared, and these are just the ones I know; there may be more. The strategy is sometimes flimsy, as when at Portsmouth, women greeting a boatload of sailors on leave from a warship have their petticoats blown up by the wind. Sometimes, Rowlandson observes a decorum of his own. Thus, in his fine drawing *George III and Queen Charlotte Driving through Deptford*, the bulk of the vast coach pushing its way through a crowded street has forced a young woman off her horse. But in deference to royalty, only her legs are shown, her bottom somehow remaining covered. One of his greatest drawings, which appears in various versions, is called *The Exhibition Stare Case*. In those days the

Royal Academy annual summer exhibition, attended by all
society, was held in Somerset House. Access to the main rooms
was by a steep, curving staircase. Rowlandson spotted that if
someone fell at the top, while a mass of people was trying to
ascend the staircase, a domino effect would follow, and society ladies' bottoms would be exposed wholesale. In the best
version, at Yale, no fewer than four ladies' bottoms are fully
revealed, and other ladies are showing their legs. The sheer
artistry and ingenuity of this drawing are phenomenal, worthy
of a better cause, some might say. But what better cause can
there be of keeping generations of people harmlessly amused?
In about 1825, for reasons I have never been able to discover,
ladies, followed in time by respectable middle-class, and then
working-class, women, started to wear drawers, thus joining
the ballerinas and the whores. Perhaps this was one of the reasons Rowlandson gave up drawing at this time: "Othello's
occupation's gone!"

# CHAPTER FIVE

# DICKENS: NOTHING SO ODD AS LIFE

C HARLES DICKENS (1812–1870) was the most
successful comic in history. It is true he was many other
things, for he was protean. But it was as a comic writer that
he climbed to the top at the age of twenty-four, and it is as a
comic writer he remains there. Edgar Allan Poe first hailed
Dickens as a "genius" when the bound copies of *Sketches by
Boz* reached America in 1836. But the real breakthrough with
the public took place in England when the fourth number of
*The Pickwick Papers* appeared, introducing Sam Weller. Hitherto, the project was a failure. The idea was to use the skills
of a sporting artist named Robert Seymour to provide a connected series of prints. Dickens was hired to write the letter-
press. But Seymour shot himself, and Dickens had to take over
the whole business, with new illustrators, first R. W. Buss, then
"Phiz" (H. K. Brown). The third number made a dismal sale

of only five hundred copies. Once Weller appeared, sales shot up to fifty thousand. This was a completely new phenomenon. Sir Walter Scott's largest sale in monthly numbers had been thirteen thousand. *The Pickwick Papers* also sold well in book form, despite the fact so many people had bought the monthly parts—many bought both. It continued to sell throughout the remainder of Dickens's life, thirty-three years, and in the fifteen years after his death in 1870, of the five million copies of his novels sold, over one million were *Pickwick*.

The tale sold on its humor, nothing else. There was nothing else. And the fact that its sales took off as soon as Sam Weller appeared makes us look closely at why he appealed to such a large number of people. Broadly speaking, humor is a matter of chaos or character. Dickens hated chaos, and rarely if ever used it as a principle of humor. The fact that his father led a chaotic life of borrowing and debt, and so was shut up in the Marshalsea prison (the young Charles Dickens with him for a time) overshadowed all Dickens's memories and filled him with dread and bitterness. Chaos to him was the bitter enemy of happiness, and inconceivable as the machinery of laughter. Both in fiction and in real life he strongly endorsed order. Thus, in *David Copperfield*, Aunt Betsey Trotwood, in calling out "Marta, donkeys!," which led to the expulsion of the dirty donkey-boys from the precious green sward in front of her neat cottage, was asserting the Order Principle. There are countless such episodes in the novels. Again, when Dickens held public Christmas celebrations at his Kentish house, Gad's Hill Place, inviting two thousand of the locals to jollification, feasting, and sports, he had handbills printed saying, "Mr. Dickens puts everyman upon his honour to assist in preserving order." Dickens led an orderly life himself, of hard work and hard playtime organized to enable him to work even harder; and it is a fact that all his villains—Fagin, Carker, Silas Wegg, Uriah Heep, Ralph Nickleby, etc.—were in one way or another enemies of order, striving to overthrow it. Two of his greatest novels, *A Tale of Two Cities* and *Barnaby Rudge*, present disorder as the impersonal villain. Equally, his benevolent comic characters, such as Micawber, always at heart stand for order, as when he annunciates the doctrine of financial order: "Annual income twenty pounds, annual expenditure nineteen, nineteen-six, result happiness. Annual income twenty pounds, annual expenditure twenty pounds and sixpence, result misery."

No: Dickens was not a comic who raised a laugh by creating chaos. He was the other type: the comic who relies upon individual character. He looked at the mass of humanity and plucked out of it the egregious and the eccentric for our delight. These oddities often do weird things, like the Gentleman in Small Clothes (*Nicholas Nickleby*), who hurled vegetables into Mrs. Nickleby's garden. But they chiefly *said* things. Dickens's humor was overwhelmingly verbal. Thus what we remember, and relish, about the Small Clothes gent, is his baffling remark "All is gas and gaiters." When Dickens first hit the public jackpot with *Pickwick*, it was the Wellerisms which rang in the ear. Sam was ingenious in his innocent worldly wisdom, and quick at doing things, but his comedy was vocal. It had a peculiar, almost invariable style, a saying followed by the occasion on which it was said. Thus: "I hope our acquaintance may be a long 'un, as the gen'l'm'n said to the fi'pun'note." And: "Out wiv it, as the father said to the child wen he swallowed a farden." And: "Anythin' for a quiet life, as the man said ven he took the sitivation at the lighthouse." And: "Avay vith melin-cholly, as the little boy said ven his school missus died." And: "Now we look compact and comfortable, as the father said ven he cut his little boy's head off to cure him o' squintin'." I have counted thirty-eight Wellerisms of this kind, and there are probably more.

Weller's power to amuse readers reinforced the appearance of Jingle, who preceded him by two chapters and likewise ex-isted by his peculiar manner of speaking. Dickens based Jingle on the pattern of a stand-up comic named Charles Matthews Sr. whose "At Home" act he saw often, though he also used a certain Potter, law-clerk in the offices of Ellis and Blackmore, whose mannerisms delighted his colleagues. Jingle's staccato speeches and anecdotes were striking—"Kent, Sir—everybody knows Kent—apples, cherries, hops, and women"—and often gruesome: "Heads, heads, take care of your heads. . . . Five children—mother—tall lady, eating sandwiches—forgot the arch—crash—knock—children look round—mother's head off—sandwich in her hand—no mouth to put it in—head of a family off—shocking, shocking!"

Indeed both Weller and Jingle employed the gruesome touch habitually. Weller, in particular, liked decapitation sto-ries: "It's over, and can't be helped, and that's one consolation, as they always say in Turkey, ven they cut the wrong man's head off." Or: "The wictim of connubiality, as Bluebeard's Domestic Chaplain said, with a tear of pity, ven he buried him." Nearly half his stories involve death by violence. But we laugh all the same, indeed all the more. It is all theater, Grand Guignol, perhaps, but on a domestic scale, and no one is ever hurt on the reader's side of the footlights.

What helped to launch Dickens as a humorist, and keep him afloat, was the fact that his jokes were classless, or rather embraced all classes, except the highest, and sexless—that is, they transcended gender. That is what struck people about *Pickwick*. The authoress Miss Mary Russell Mitford wrote (June 1837) to an Irish friend, "A lady might read it all aloud; and it is so graphic, so individual and so true, that you curtsey to all the people as if you met them in the street! All the boys and girls talk his fun." Sir Benjamin Brodie, the leading physician, took *Pickwick* with him in his carriage, for reading between calls. Lord Denman read it while waiting for juries to reach their verdict. John Ruskin and his father took it in turns to read aloud. Ruskin said he knew much of it by heart. Macaulay said the same. The novelist Mrs. Gaskell, in Cranford, described it being read in country villages. There were Pickwick Hats and China Pickwicks. Evidence exists to show it was read by chimney sweeps and serving maids, by the butcher's boy and the footman. The tales were not genteel, by any means. Led by Pickwick himself, who gets incapably drunk on one occasion, the characters virtually all drink, including and especially the militant teetotal preacher, Mr. Stiggins. One authority calculates there are 295 instances in *Pickwick* in which spirituous or malt liquor is taken. Consumption of alcohol is a perpetual theme, with infinite variations, of the book. It was, as Dickens intended, a powerful antidote to the tracts of the temperance lobby. Yet readers found its moral tone, if not exactly uplifting, at least comforting, especially as it progressed. The *Edinburgh Review* observed, "The novel of high spirits became the novel of good spirits." Thomas Hood felt it "drove to the soul of goodness in things evil," and wrote of "The Goodness of Pickwickedness." Speaking for American readers, Washington Irving hailed Pickwick himself as "the Quixote of commonplace life, and as with the Don, we begin by laughing at him and end by loving him." This was Dickens's intention, as he said in the preface to the first printing of *Pickwick* in book form: he wrote that he hoped the work would make the reader "think better of his fellow men and look upon the brighter and more kindly side of human nature."

As his work advanced, and matured, Dickens learned to alternate comedy and pathos, to make readers sob as well as laugh. None did this more effectively than *David Copperfield*, perhaps the most personal of his novels and certainly his favorite. Lord John Russell, while prime minister, read it to his wife and "we cried . . . until we were ashamed." When *Copperfield* appeared as a serial in New York, a small boy aged seven, Henry James, supposed to be in bed, hid under a table to listen. As the cruelty of Mr. Murdstone was exposed, he "broke into sobs of sympathy," was discovered, and sent upstairs. His admiration of Dickens, at this stage, and for long after, was unbounded, and when he first met the author in 1867, found him "extremely handsome" and was filled with "a curious and overwhelming tenderness," seeing him as the embodiment of "the sublimity of mastership" in writing.

If *Pickwick* was the quintessence of verbal tricks and extravagances to raise laughter, and later writings brought in all the other emotions to keep the readership first attracted by fun, Dickens never dropped his gift for patter. If Franklin invented the one-liner, Dickens created the equally characteristic British device, the verbal running gag. It is, indeed, to be found in Shakespeare, notably in *Henry IV, Part One*, where the waiter at the Boar's Head tavern, Francis, gets repeated laughs with his "Anon, anon, Sir!" But Dickens turned it into a comic institution. Mr. Dick, in *David Copperfield*, has his "King Charles's head." Mrs. General in *Little Dorrit* repeats her elocutionary litany: "Papa, potatoes, poultry, prunes and prison—especially prunes and prison." Captain Cuttle, in *Dombey and Son*, advises, "When found, make a note of." Micawber "waits for something to turn up," and his wife swears "I will never desert Mr. Micawber." Mrs. Gummidge, also in *Copperfield*, repeats "I'm a lone, lorn creeter, and everything goes contrairy with me," to which Peggotty responds: "She's been thinkin' of the old 'un." Then there is the signature line of Toots in *Dombey*: "It's of no consequence," and Guppy in *Bleak House*: "There are chords in the human mind." Then there is Mr. Mantalini in *Nickleby*, and his mangle: "I am always turning the mangle. I am perpetually turning, like a dem'd old horse in a demnition mill. My life is one dem'd horrid grind." He also gets repeated chuckles by calling his long-suffering wife "my essential juice of pineapple." Then there is the humbugging minister Mr. Chadband in *Bleak House*, and his "truth," brilliantly introduced by Dickens as "A large yellow man, with a fat smile and a general appearance of having too much train oil in his system . . . who never speaks without putting up his great hand, as delivering a token to his hearers that he is going to edify them." He has a running device of asking rhetorical questions: "What is peace? Is it war? No. Is it strife? No." His speech rhythms are essentially prelatical. "You are a human boy, my young friend. A human boy. O glorious to be a human boy!"

O running stream of sparkling joy!
To be a soaring human boy!

He introduces his running-gag line with a fine pulpit flourish: "It is the ray of rays, the sun of suns, the moon of moons, the star of stars. It is the light of Terewth!" Then there is the carter in *Copperfield* with "Barkis is willin'"—a real stroke of genius, that. Even animals have running gags, like Grip the Raven, in *Barnaby Rudge*, who sings "Polly put the kettle on, and we'll all have tea." Someone wrote a musical ditty for these words, and it attracted the ear of Lord Beaverbrook, the masterful and mischievous newspaper owner. He did not recognize many tunes, but he knew this one, and he would sing it to his editors with his own words, exhorting them

Sow the seeds of discord!
Sow the seeds of discord!
Sow the seeds of discord!
And we'll all have fun.

Dickens would not have liked that. It went against the
principle of order. And experience had taught him to distrust
publishers of all sorts. Grip was based on a real raven, of whom
Dickens was fond, but who was found dead after eating a meal
of lead-based white paint.

Some of Dickens's creatures have not merely one running
gag but several. Indeed they are composed of words rather than
flesh. In *Martin Chuzzlewit*, Mrs. Gamp, one of Dickens's most
successful creations, who gave her surname to the language, is
not exactly an immaterial presence—quite the contrary—but
she is essentially a vehicle for her peculiar observations and tor-
ture of words. "The torters of the Imposition shouldn't make
me own I did." "This Piljian's Projiss of a mortal wale." "Rich
folks may ride on camels, but it ain't so easy for 'em to see
out of a needle's eye. That's my comfort, and I 'opes I knows
it." "The Antwerp paquet-boat, and I wish it was in Jonadge's
belly, I do." "Bless the babe, and save the mother is my mortar.
But I makes so free as to add to that, Don't try no impogician
with the Nuss, for she will not abear it." " 'Mrs. Harris,' I says,
'leave the bottle on the chimney piece, and don't ask me to
take non, but let me put my lips to it when I am so dispoged.' "
"I am but a poor woman, and I earns my livin' hard. Therefore I *do* require it, which I make confession, to be brought

reg'lar and draw'n mild." "Some people may be Rooshans, and others may be Prooshans. They are so born and will please themselves. Them which is of other natures thinks different." Part of Mrs. Gamp's running gag was her conversations with her friend Mrs. Harris, which tended to be for her own glorification. " 'Sairey,' said Mrs. Harris, 'you are gold which has passed the furnage.' " Mrs. Harris never makes an appearance, however, and not everyone was sure she existed. Eventually Betsy Prig came out with the blasphemous accusation "I don't believe there's no sich a person." This almost killed Mrs. Gamp: "The words Betsy Prig spoke of Mrs. Harris, lambs could not forgive, nor worms forget." But Mrs. Gamp was not long daunted: "What a blessed thing it is—living in a wale—to be contented." And: "The families I've had, if all was know'd and credit done where credit's doo, would take a week to christen at St. Polge's fontin." According to Lockhart, Mrs. Gamp was based upon a nurse who attended an invalid lady Dickens knew. Her common habit, in the sick room, was to rub her nose along a tall fender. Her famous "gig umbrella" was "in colour like a faded leaf, except where a circular patch of a lively blue had been dexterously let in at the top."

Though Dickens rejected chaos as a source of fun, he was keen on mystery, not only for drama and melodrama but for humor too. He liked dark utterances. After all, what *are* "gas and gaiters"? The entire speech by the Gentleman in Small Clothes is not exactly clarifying. He says, on seeing Miss La Creevy, and to the consternation of Mrs. Nickleby: "My love, my life, my bride, my peerless beauty, she is come at last—at last!—and all is gas and gaiters!" We are no wiser, and Dickens never explained. There is also the mysterious case of the woman known only as "Mr. F's Aunt." She lived with Flora Finching (in *Little Dorrit*), who always referred to her late husband as "Mr. F." His aunt's "major characteristics were extreme severity and grim taciturnity, sometimes interrupted by a propensity to offer remarks in a deep warning voice, which, being totally uncalled for by anything said by anybody, and traceable to no association of ideas, confounded and terrified the mind." Such was her remark: "There's milestones on the Dover Road." This is not exactly a running gag, but it is a saying one remembers, and ponders (as Dickens intended). The words are more important than the person, about whom, really, we know nothing, except her name, and even that is enigmatic. A similar character is the Fat Boy (in *Pickwick*), and his remark "Missus, I wants to make your flesh creep." We know nothing about him either, except he is no longer exactly a boy, more a young man imprisoned in his own flesh and in his superannuated role as page. Frank Richards, of *The Magnet*, had him in mind when he created Greyfriars School (1908) and Billy Bunter, "the Fat Owl of the Remove."

Another occult figure, though we know rather more about him, is Grandfather Smallweed in *Bleak House*. He is a paralyzed usurer, who lives in a basket chair propped up by cushions, which frequently have to be plumped up to make him more comfortable and upright. He gets honest Trooper George into his clutches, and so becomes part of the machinery of the novel's immensely complicated plot. What distinguishes

Smallweed is that his tiny body is entirely composed of malice. Much of it is directed at his silent and imbecile wife, whose maiden name presumably was Krook, since her brother was so-called, and he is another cog (though a defunct one) in the machinery. Smallweed throws cushions at his wife, and calls her "a brimstone chatterer," though she never says a word. This is an example of the way in which Dickens, who never used an actual swear word, for fear of offending women readers, invents harmless expletives in order to convey the impression of dire profanity. "Brimstone chatterer" is thus Smallweed's running gag.

Dickens's ability to extract laughter by hovering precariously on the borderline between mystery and evil is one of his many comic gifts, as is his willingness to turn disfigurement, disability, and various forms of mental retardation into sources of humor. (Whether he could conceivably have been a comic novelist, or indeed a writer at all, in an age of Political Correctness is a point worth pondering.) Silas Wegg in *Our Mutual Friend* is a one-legged villain who is paid half a crown a night to read Gibbon to Mr. Boffin, the millionaire dustman. He charges extra for poetry for "when a person comes to grind off poetry night after night, it is but right he should be paid for its weakening effect on the brain." He also requires liquid refreshment: "I generally reads in gin and water. It mellers the organ, Sir." To what extent Wegg can actually read is a moot point, for he believes the book to be called *The Decline and Fall Off the Rooshian Empire*. And when exposed, he has a brilliant exit line: "With the single exception of the salary I renounce the whole and total sitiwation." Wegg's missing leg would, in our age, rule him out for service as a villain, even a minor one. But in Dickens's comic universe, disablement was often a cause of turpitude. To some extent he seems to have shared the medieval belief that deformity was the work of the devil—a belief going back to the Old Testament and the book of Deuteronomy which taught that priests, especially "high" ones, must be whole and perfect in body. Wegg, be it noted, was based on a well-known character who in Dickens's youth kept a ballad and gingerbread stall near Cavendish Square. It is important to realize that very few of Dickens's grotesques, however outlandish, were creatures purely of his imagination. There was usually a prototype he had seen, met, or heard of. A close reading of the newspapers and magazines of the years 1820–1840 reveals that the seemingly bizarre world of his fiction was also the world in which he was brought up. His humor, seemingly far-fetched, sprang from the streets of London he walked.

Where, I think, Dickens was truly inventive was in his nomenclature. No other novelist had quite the same poetical ingenuity, which in a way binds together his entire opus. Copperfield and Nickleby, Dorrit and Chuzzlewit, Swiveller, Tappertit, and Jarndyce, are all personal markers in a land of fairy tale; yet real too. Many of these names, however bizarre, are to be found in parish registers of the time. Yet they all have the Dickens stamp. Quilp (*Old Curiosity Shop*) was, it seems, a real person, and his dwelling has been identified, though since demolished. But who was Mrs. Jiniwin, Mrs. Quilp's mother, "known to be laudibly shrewish in her disposition"? Who were

Dick Swiveller and Kit Nubbles? Miss Mowcher was another misfit, a dwarf. She had a client named Pyegrave. Then there is Uncle Pumblechook in *Great Expectations*, and Sophy Wackles, Swiveller's first love, "a fresh, good humoured, buxom girl of twenty," whom he throws over, and then is mortified to see her make a successful marriage to a market-gardener named Cheggs. There is Chevy Slyme, a minor Chuzzlewit relative, who has "the peculiarity of being always round the corner." He has a friend named Tigg. Curious names are often linked. Dot Perrybingle's personal maid is named Tilly Slowboy. Bayham Badger, a doctor (*Bleak House*) is married to a woman whose previous husbands were Captain Swosser and Professor Dingo. Captain Boldwig and Dr. Slammer, Sladdery, Cornelius Brook Dingwall, the pilot Bulph and beadle Bung, Mrs. Wititterley of Cadogan Place (where I once lived), described as "the connecting link between the aristocratic pavements of Belgrave Square and the barbarism of Chelsea," Major Hannibal Chollop, Trotty Veck, Conkey Chickweed—antihero of a tale "narrated with much gusto by Mr. Blathers"—Dr. Clatter, Clickett (Mrs. Micawber's maid, "with a habit of snorting," who informed David Copperfield she was an "orfling"), Jerry Cruncher, a "Resurection Man who took a great interest in funerals," Sir Dingleby Dabber, and Dick Datchery ("I am an idle dog who lives upon my means") are just some of the three thousand or so characters who adorn Dickens's fictions.

He took trouble over the names of inanimate objects too, especially places. There is the Slamjam Coffee House, in the story "Somebody's Luggage," and the Three Cripples Inn, favorite pub of Bill Sikes in *Oliver Twist*. The *Uncommercial Traveller* describes St. Ghastly Grim, based on St. Olave's in Hart Street, where Samuel Pepys is buried. Plashwater weir and its mill lock, scene of Bradley Headstone's fatal fight with Roger Riderhood (*Our Mutual Friend*) is based on Hurley Lock near Henley. The Pig and Tinderbox Inn is another Dickens invention, as is the Willing Mind tavern, in *Copperfield*, and the Blue Lion and Stomachwarmer in *Sketches by Boz*. Baker's Trap, described in the *Uncommercial Traveller* as a sunny bridge "over some dark locks and dirty water," was a favorite place for suicides—Baker being the local coroner. This was a real trap, near Wapping. The Anglo-Bengalee Disinterested Loan and Life Assurance Company, which features in *Chuzzlewit*, had a paid-up capital "of a two, and as many noughts as the printer can get into the line." The Tilted Wagon inn is yet another invented pub: Dickens complained that "real inn names are so peculiar it is hard to outdo them." Indeed the George and Vulture inn, which figures in *Pickwick*, actually existed, and is still there in Lombard Street.

Although Dickens looked to people for his humor, he sometimes (like Kipling) anthropomorphized things and got his laughs that way. Thus, in *A Christmas Carol*, the knocker on the front door of Scrooge's chambers turns into the face of his former partner, Marley, who had been dead seven years. Dickens made the weather live too. Thus, in the opening paragraph of *Bleak House*, he creates "implacable November weather"— "As much mud in the streets, as if the waters had but newly retired from the face of the earth, and it would not be wonderful to meet a Megalosaurus, forty feet long or so, waddling like an elephantine lizard up Holborn Hill." Even the lighted gas, he adds, "peering out of the fog," has "a haggard and unwilling look." At the opening of *Great Expectations* (the best chapter Dickens ever wrote), the tombstone and its letters come to life for little Pip. And when he has stolen the savory pork pie, and other "vittles," to give to the escaped convict Magwich, and hurries across the marches to deliver them, his feelings of guilt make the entire landscape come to life and gaze at him accusingly. "One black ox, with a white cravat on—who even had to my awakened conscience something of a clerical air—fixed me so obstinately with his eyes, and moved his blunt head round in such an accusatory manner as I moved round, that I blubbered out to him 'I couldn't help it, Sir! It wasn't for myself I took it!'"

Dickens made people laugh in his works. He made them laugh in his person. He was an actor of professional standard, and could have made a fortune on the stage just as surely as he made one by his books. Indeed his readings netted him £60,000. He concentrates on dramatic episodes and pathos— the murder of Nancy and the flight of Bill Sikes in *Oliver Twist*, and the death of Little Nell in *The Old Curiosity Shop*, for instance—because he liked to see ladies carried out of the auditorium in a dead faint. But he did the comic turns too, from *Pickwick*, *Copperfield*, and *Bleak House*. He also did comic turns in his many charity shows. He made his friends (Clarkson Stanfield, Macready, Maclise, Forster, Wilkie Collins, etc.) laugh continually at their all-male dinners and excursions. He made his family, especially Mary and Kate, laugh at Gad's Hill Place. He was funny even when alone. Kate described creeping into his study unobserved and watching him compose. He would write a paragraph, get up and act it, in front of the looking glass, practicing the facial expressions especially, laugh, then sit down to write again. The process was repeated many times. "He felt his bosom full of jokes, and he had to let them out." This externalization of inner comic demons was a central part of his character. And unlike most stage comics, Dickens was not a victim of melancholy because his comic personality was only part of his act, most of which went into writing. He was too busy, always, to find time for sadness. As the twelve massive volumes of the Pilgrim Edition of his *Letters* (14,252 in all) show, his life was packed tight with activity even on "holiday." But the days were punctuated by modest doses of alcohol, which acted as his comic detonator.

It is not usually grasped how important alcohol was in Dickens's life. Not that he was an alcoholic: quite the contrary. He detested uncontrolled drinking. No one ever described him as drunk. But wine, spirits, and malt liquors were regular items of existence for him, oiling the precise machines of his busy life, work, and pleasure, and linking him to his vast acquaintance. As soon as he became a success, aged twenty-four, he set up a cellar, and began to stock it with a wide range of high-quality liquor. In all his houses, the cellar was, after his writing room, the most important part of the building. It was well and fully stocked, with wine and spirits in barrels, tins, and bottles. It was always jealously guarded and locked up, with endless precautions taken about the keys. Having a superb cellar was perhaps for Dickens the most significant sign that he had "arrived," had put all his childhood firmly behind him. But it had to be protected. He was paranoid on this point. From the United States, where he was reading, he wrote to his sister-in-law Georgiana:

> I have been constantly thinking about that cellar key, and I will tell you how we will keep it. Order from Chubbs's man one of the ordinary little iron cash boxes to keep it in. To that cash box have made two keys, both electro-typed gold. Of those keys you shall always wear one, and I will always wear the other, and the box itself shall be kept, not in your room but in mine, in some drawer that we will settle upon. Then, I think, we must be safe.

Dickens was not only worried his cellar might be entered by thieves but that they were conspiring in some way to interfere with the liquor in its containers. A similarly paranoid letter was addressed to a well-known firm of distillers:

> Mr. Charles Dickens sends his compliments to Messrs. Seager Evans & Co., and begs them to test the accompanying bottle of gin drawn from their cask this morning. It appears to Mr. Dickens to have neither the right strength nor flavour, and he thinks it must have been tampered with at the Railway. When the cask was tapped at Gad's Hill on Saturday, it was observed to be particularly full.

Dickens bought in quantity: casks, tuns, and barrels not just of beer but of whiskey, gin, rum, and wine. One order to his wine merchant was for six casks of whiskey at £35 8s. each, two barrels of sherry, two barrels of red wine, and a quantity of champagne—"six dozen quarts and six dozen pints." He got his brandy in large bottles, by the dozen. A letter shows he sent his sister "A Dozen of fine old brandy, which I hope will do you good." Dickens had a comforting belief in the medicinal qualities of alcoholic liquor. He described with relish a "restorative mixture" he discovered in America, to be taken in bed before rising, and which he called "An Eye-Opener." Another with which he dosed himself for his "catargh," was known to him as a Rocky Mountain Sneezer. It was made up of brandy, rum, bitters, and fresh snow.

While traveling and working flat out in America (and also on his later British reading tours) he devised for himself a curious diet which he described, in a letter to his daughter Mary, as his "system":

At seven in the morning, in bed, a tumbler of new cream and two tablespoonfuls of rum. At twelve a sherry cobbler and a biscuit. At three [dinner time], a pint of champagne. At five minutes to eight, an egg beaten up with a glass of sherry. Between the parts [of his readings] the strongest beef tea that can be made, drunk hot. At a quarter past ten, soup and anything to drink that I can fancy. I don't eat more than half a pound of solid food in the twenty-four hours, if so much.

Dickens needed the stimulus of alcohol, of different kinds, high quality but in modest (often small) amounts, to keep his comic and imaginative faculties in constant motion. He was never tipsy, never slurred his words in the smallest degree, and never said anything he later regretted. All was orderly, regular, and calm. It was, as he said, a "system." But it required alcohol rather as a car requires lubricating fluid. His huge energy and animal spirits supplied, as it were, the gasoline to drive the car forward. This is an interesting case, and helps to explain why drinking alcohol occupies such a persistent place in his novels and gives them an odd kind of unity.

CHAPTER SIX

# TOULOUSE-LAUTREC: MASTER-MONSTER

WHAT IS FUNNY about Henri de Toulouse-Lautrec (1864–1901)? And what is funny about his work? These are interesting but difficult questions. The second is easier to answer than the first. He is like one of those artists of Balzac's *La comédie humaine*, and what he pictures, with extraordinary visual accuracy and in superb color, is the human comedy of France, and above all Paris, in the 1880s and 1890s, an especially interesting time. In depicting this human *comédie*, which of course enshrines tragedy at its center—the comedy, as always, is peripheral, though obtrusively so—Lautrec is essentially French. Indeed he is the quintessentially Gallic comedian, if a painter can be so described, more so than Honoré Daumier, the only one to run him close. His work did not, of course, depict the whole of France. The peasants, who made up 75 percent of the population, are scarcely there at all, and the industrial workers are invisible. But what could then be seen on the streets of Paris, notably Montmartre, and behind the walls of its houses, is shown to us in staggering intimacy and an almost religious fidelity to the truth. We wonder, we smile, we laugh, we are entertained: the delight does not wear off; on the contrary, it intensifies the more we study what he did, and learn about the people he shows us. He was not just a great artist but an inspired impresario, like Diaghilev.

The comparison with the audacious Russian is apt, for just as Diaghilev created (from superb material it is true) dancers like Nijinski and Pavlova, so Lautrec made his characters. It is important to grasp that he was a man of considerable intelligence, wide reading, extreme sensitivity in some ways, and massive strength of character. He took people and essentialized them in his work. To borrow a phrase from Shakespeare, he plucked out the heart of their mystery. It was not caricature, though it employed all the skills of the trade: it was truth telling, but with a difference. Much of it was painful as well as comic truth, and some of it truth never before told at all.

He was able to do this partly because of his own tragicomic person. He was a hideously but also laughably deformed dwarf. We tend to push this aside because his was a classic case of triumph over tragedy, a life of pain, shame, and self-degradation redeemed by a mass of creative work of superlative quality. Though he failed to reach his thirty-seventh birthday, and was often too ill to work at all, the quantity of his oeuvre is impressive, and nearly all of it is good. He was born to wealth and rank. Most men with his afflictions would have done nothing with their lives save hide and brood. He came from one of France's grandest families which had once possessed the fine city of Toulouse, and still owned many thousands of rich acres. But it had a fatal propensity to inbreed. Henri and four of his cousins were the victims of a doubling of a recessive gene carried by both his parents and his uncle and aunt. The effects varied. One female cousin merely suffered from pain and weakness in her legs. But three others were badly deformed, and dwarfs as well. One of them spent her entire life in a large wicker baby carriage.

Henri was a little more fortunate. Fragility at the growth end of his bones hindered normal development and caused pain, deformation, and weakness in his skeletal structure. This condition became obvious in adolescence. It baffled the doctors and proved impossible to treat. As an adult, he had a normal torso but his knock-kneed legs were comically short and his stocky arms had huge hands with fingers like clubs. His bones were fragile and would break easily, often without apparent cause. He limped, had very large nostrils, bulbous lips, a thickened tongue, and a speech impediment. He sniffed continually and drooled at the mouth.

His disabilities, however, did not affect his brain, eyesight, or hand control. He possessed astonishing artistic skills, and once he discovered this, and honed them by training, he determined to live and work in Paris, in the open as it were, and seek a living and fame by his skill. Paris was then the world center of art, and astonishingly accommodating socially to artists. He instinctively grasped that, denied normality, let alone happiness, he could come closer to a normal life, and glimpses of happiness, in Paris than anywhere else. He had a surprising amount of energy. He was also capable of a sexual life. With the exception of the model and painter Suzanne Valadon, his sexuality was lavished on prostitutes, usually casual ones. But his sexual escapades were as rich and varied as Paris could provide, and like many other small men he had the useful reputation of possessing a monstrous member. With a good deal of aristocratic hauteur, Lautrec did not allow himself to be inhibited by his appearance. Indeed he was photographed surprisingly often, painting, standing in front of his canvases, once with a naked model with an extraordinary quantity of pubic hair, and often naked himself, or in drag, and on one occasion defecating on a beach. He was in fact a reckless fellow, a bit of an exhibitionist, as well as a notorious voyeur (as all great painters must be).

Unfortunately, his reckless but in some ways joyous way of life, in the studio, the café, and the brothel, compounded his inherited disabilities. From his mid-twenties he was a serious alcoholic. Worse, he caught syphilis. So of course did many artists and writers in the nineteenth century. As Gustave Flaubert put it, "Everybody has it, more or less." In Lautrec's case it is clearly reflected in his work. Dégas, commenting on his representation of the female form, noted, "Ses femmes puent la vérole à plein nez"—his women stink of syphilis. He was strongly attracted to redheaded women, and he caught the disease from a tart named Rosa la Rouge, despite being warned she was infected. He was treated with mercury, the only way in those days that the malady might, with luck, be arrested, even cured. This turned his teeth black, and distressed him. It is significant he never allowed himself to be photographed with his mouth open.

This, then, was the man. What of the comic artist? It is useful to distinguish between his treatment of men and women. To Lautrec, men were always comic, even those he loved. One of the few aristocrats to whom he was close was his cousin Gabriel, who rejoiced under the surname Tapié de Céleyran. This boulevardier and ardent theatergoer was tall, pear-shaped, with dark hair and moustache, and a big nose with pince-nez on its bridge. Lautrec often drew him, and did a magnificent painting of him prowling down the corridor of the Comédie-Française, cigarette in hand, with a hubbub of prowling women behind him. He contrived to show that Tapié could look willowy and baggy at the same time. Lautrec, who loved peculiar animals, especially anteaters, called his cousin Tapir la Scélerat (Tapir the Scoundrel), one of many nicknames for him he devised.

Lautrec regarded all Englishmen as comic in one way or another. He liked to show them as rich, innocent or ignorant, lascivious, and easy meat for the tramp-girls of the boulevards. They were tall, fair-haired, blue-eyed, and with big moustaches. These milords or haw-haws, as he called them, were jolly and decorative characters in his comic strip of Montmartre nightlife. For his model archetype he picked on Charles Conder, whom he drew and painted many times. In fact Conder was not a rich English aristo but a painter, and eventually a good one. Moreover he was an Australian and belligerently proud of the fact. But he was flattered by Lautrec's interest. Oscar Wilde, on the other hand, hated Lautrec's use of his face and figure, which was shown as gross, ugly, sensual, and disgusting. Lautrec of course portrayed him in his pathetic decline, after his emergence from prison when (as he put it) he "let himself go." These drawings are more caricatures than portraits, and into them Lautrec put his distaste for *le vice anglais*, refusing to accept that Wilde was an Irishman.

However the two male characters who occupied principal places in Lautrec's cast were both French and both pillars of Montmartre anti-society. Both would now be forgotten had not Lautrec immortalized them; as it is, they are comic giants. Aristide Bruant was a lower-middle-class provincial who had an astonishingly loud but tuneful voice, and he wrote his own songs. They were bitter, sentimental, often funny, blasphemous, and peppered with "bad" words and Parisian argot. When Lautrec first met him he had set up his shop in an abandoned nightclub on a rough stretch of the Boulevard de Rochechouart, at the foot of Montmartre. He called it Le Mirleton, the French word for a whistle, which also means "ditty." He advertised it as "Aristide Bruant dans son cabaret." It had wooden tables and hard benches, though there was one Louis XIII chair, in which he would sometimes sit. The drinks were chiefly beer, wine, and grog, made with Martinique rum, and the clientele were overwhelmingly working class to begin with. The songs Bruant wrote and bawled at them were aimed at a lumpen proletariat audience. But soon, quite different people came slumming to the Mirleton, to Bruant's disgust. He swore at them, and to his fury they liked it, and brought their friends. When Bruant wrote songs to insult them, and the haute bourgeoisie generally, they liked it still more. Soon, Bruant found himself a hit. Le Mirleton was packed, and he kept the door barred, peering at new arrivals through a tiny grille and deciding himself whom to let in. In 1886, Bruant's cabaret was the smartest night spot in Paris, and it was then that Lautrec went there, and immediately decided Bruant was a perfect subject for his art.

Bruant was tall (six feet) and burly. He dressed in black trousers, and black corduroy jacket, a red flannel shirt, and huge black boots of the kind worn by sewer cleaners. He had a wide black hat and a red woolen scarf flung around his throat and over his shoulder. He also had a black cloak, which he wore when he stood in the door of his club, or marched triumphantly up and down the boulevard. He had a huge rustic walking stick, and on his (often) unwashed and un-shaven face there was a savage sneer. His expression conveyed: "I despise you, all the more for coming here and making me rich." He saw himself as a poor artist, and felt the painters who flocked to Montmartre, and worked in the streets and garrets, were his confreres. He hung their paintings on the walls of his cabaret, for sale. Nearly all were of local whores, another way to *épater la bourgeoisie.* By the time Lautrec came, the club had a sign over its door: "Le Mirleton; rendez-vous pour eux qui cherchent être abusés." It opened at ten and he sang until two, encouraging the clients to join in the choruses. Once the place became fashionable, he served nothing except beer in small glasses called *galopins*. He drank it with the customers, sitting at their tables. As he put it, "I praised soldiers, tolerated members of the Académie, was rude to the boulevardiers, poured hate on the politicians, treated dukes like Cossacks and patronized kings." He also published a periodical, *Le Mirleton*, about twenty times a year, and sold it at the club, with new poems and *éclats d'esprit* by unknown writers.

He adored Lautrec, and when he came to the club would stop singing, and shout, "Silence, messieurs et madames— here is the great painter, Toulouse-Lautrec." Lautrec did posters for him, some of the best he ever designed, and helped to make him famous. He also did many sketches of the monster. In return, Bruant bought his paintings, including the brilliant and painful portrait of a woman with a hangover, *La gueule de bois*, and displayed them on the club walls. It was a meeting of minds, of two men who saw themselves as outsiders and outcasts of society but in fact were its pets. And in his drawings and posters of Bruant, Lautrec conveys perfectly the ferocious humor which was his speciality.

The other great man in Lautrec's Montmartre pleiad was Valentin le Désossé. He worked, or rather amused himself (he was not paid to perform, having some kind of regular job in the daytime), up the hill in a club called Le Moulin de la Galette, near Lautrec's studio in the Rue Lepic. It had been a flour mill until the siege of Paris, and in the 1870s became a working-class resort for dancing in the evenings, and on Sunday afternoons. It acquired a ballroom lined with glass, and a garden where masses of girls—maidservants, laundresses, seamstresses, and hatmakers, delivery girls, and nursemaids, plus a few young men—danced under the trees. There were no professional performers and even the band was mainly composed of amateurs. Anyone could come along and dance for a few *sous* (cents or pennies) or even perform if they were good enough to play in tune and keep time. It was the way the poor of Paris entertained themselves: cheaply and uproariously. This was the scene, in 1876, when Renoir, who was still a young man with dazzling talent, painted his beautiful *Bal du Moulin de la Galette*. Lautrec saw this painting in the Durand-Ruel art gallery, and went to the club to sketch himself. He found that some of the working girls, who were pretty and good natural dancers, did (as it were) solo turns, dancing the quadrille, ending in a *chatut* in which they kicked their legs high and exposed their underclothes. They hoped to be spotted by owners of nightclubs and given professional engagements which could hoist them out of poverty. Some of them were daring and shameless, and the news of their abandoned dancing got around and attracted well-heeled gentlemen from all over the city. The owners were able to put up their prices, serve fancy drinks, and refuse admission to the male toughs, who originally kept away the nicer girls.

By the mid-1880s the Moulin, like Bruant's Mirleton, was becoming fashionable, and the dancing girls were expert. This is where Valentin came in. He was a natural dancer. His name was Jacques Renaudin and he came from a "good" family. He had a comfortable flat in the eighth arrondissement and stables where he kept horses, and every morning went for a ride in the Bois. But he loved dancing and bohemian company and within a few years of frequenting La Galette he was put in charge of rehearsing the more talented girls. By 1885 the good ones were on the payroll and Valentin picked out promising new ones to join the chorus. That is the origin of Lautrec's wonderful painting, done in 1889, *Dressages des nouvelles, par Valentin le Désossé au Moulin-Rouge.*

Valentin was called "désossé," slang for boneless, because he was double-jointed in both legs and could perform the splits and other contortions in the most astonishing way. The only photo of him which survives shows him leg-splitting flat on the floor. In the photo, he in no way resembles Lautrec's painting, and it may have been taken when he was much younger. The Valentin Lautrec knew and painted was very tall, middle-aged (fortyish), gaunt, and unsmiling, always wearing a big top hat, perched over his brow at an angle, even when doing the most vigorous dances. His chin jutted out, his mouth was a thin, saturnine line, and he kept his hands on his hips while his legs gyrated and bent in a rubbery way. He was an astonishing figure, and Lautrec made him a central character in the human comedy of Montmartre.

Valentin raised from obscurity several girls who became paid star dancers, first in the Moulin, then at other clubs and halls. They were known by their nicknames, such as La Môme Fromage (cheesy mother), Rigolette (laughing girl), Rayon d'Or (golden sunbeam), and Grille d'Egout (grid-teeth). The most famous was La Goulue (greedy girl), whom Lautrec loved to draw and paint. She was the most shameless of the dancers in showing her legs, and sometimes danced without any underclothes at all, so that during the *chatuts* which ended each quadrille she allowed the male spectators who crowded around the dance floor when she was performing tantalizing glimpses of her pubic hair and pudenda. She was also a superb dancer. Her trouble was greed. She would eat anything they gave her, and drink too huge glasses of white wine. A photo taken of her when she first became a star shows her naked from the waist up, blond and delectable but already double chinned. She performed in some of the top venues, and must have earned a lot of money at one time. But she was sacked for being overweight. Then she set up her own show, and wrote to Lautrec (the letter survives) asking him to paint for what she called her *barraque* (dancing tent), a canvas backcloth showing her dancing with Valentin and others at the Moulin Rouge. Lautrec obliged her, and this huge, rather coarse painting, after many misadventures, survives. La Goulue's cabaret did not, however, and she gradually descended into the gutter, selling matches and ending destitute.

She is the first woman in Lautrec's splendid panorama of Montmartre characters. He showed her dancing, lifting up her skirts; drinking; being supported, drunk, on her way home; and lying in bed. He made her live, and presents her in all her charm and folly: rambunctious, joyful, gobbling everything in sight, living for the hour, giving everything she had to give without thought for the morrow, talented, a kind of bohemian genius but also ignorant and stupid. Lautrec's Goulue is the Queen of Slut, the Divine Eating-machine, the Voracious Venus, the ravenous and ravishing wanton. He enjoyed painting her as much as she enjoyed gobbling, and they moved down the slippery slope together, in step. Her real name was Louise Weber (from Alsace) and she was a strawberry blonde whose topknot-and-tail hairdo was imitated everywhere in the years of fame when Lautrec put her on the posters. It was still a topknot but bedraggled white when she ended in the gutter. By that time Lautrec was long dead and unable to help.

The woman he enjoyed painting even more than he did Goulue was the chanteuse Yvette Guilbert—I say "chanteuse" but this is by courtesy, for she was more of a diseuse to begin with, speaking her songs (which were very bawdy), until she was taught to sing them in a half-shout, half-whisper, rather like Rex Harrison in *My Fair Lady*. She was a real star, arousing tremendous electricity in a hall or theater when she walked gawkily onto center stage. When she came to London in 1898 and again in 1907 George Bernard Shaw gave her golden and vivid notices, and there is an enthusiastic description of her performances by Arthur Symons: "She suggests purity and perversity at the same time . . . the eyes of a child, of a pure, cloudless blue, shining with malicious cleverness, closed in extreme lassitude, open in surprise which empties them of all expression." She was tall, angular, extremely flat chested, with a long sharp nose and high arched eyebrows: no beauty, quite the reverse.

Lautrec fell for her immediately when he saw her perform, and their first meeting, in 1892, was a wonderful example of *la comédie humaine.* She saw him as "a dark-haired head, enormous with an empurpled face, and black face-hair, skin composed of oil and grease, a huge, double-size nose, a mouth like a sabre slash across the face, with drooping, drooling lips, purple colored—yet the eyes were beautiful, wide and enormous, radiating warmth." He, on the other hand, immediately saw her as a poster: "Inborn chastity and elegance—no flaunting or coquetry—and an intelligence that enabled her to transform herself into a living caricature, a macabre advertisement."

She immediately asked him to construct a poster of her. Thus began a long interconnection, Lautrec drawing her hundreds of times, and constructing a new visual personality on the basis of her artistry. She had originally worn long black gloves, "up to the armpits," to achieve contrast with her white, virginal dress, and underline the innocent/depraved dichotomy. Lautrec seized on the long black arms, and the extended bony fingers to make them the living symbol of her entire body. He had only to draw her arms, or even just her hands, and there was the entire Yvette Guilbert, unmistakable. He then turned to her face, and turned it into a unique combination of *jolie laide féroce*, so that if he showed it, or even part of it, peeping around a curtain at the audience, the entire woman—child and empress of vice—was immediately present. No stage creature has ever been so skillfully and mordantly reduced to elemental essentials by a great artist. She was already becoming famous when Lautrec got to work on her. But he made her into a deathless phenomenon, creating unforgettable living images which still shock and delight over a century later.

Inevitably her feelings were mixed. At first she raged: "Almighty God! By the Virgin Mary, do not make me so ugly! People say they shrieked with horror when they first saw your poster. Yes, it is art, I see it, but many do not grasp your artistry, they just pick on the ugliness. Oh, I know I am no beauty, but do not make me so totally horrible, please, I beg you." She said to him, "You are a genius in depicting deformity." He replied, "Is that surprising? Of course I am, it is my nature." Thus began a precarious friendship, based upon an edgy mutual respect. She took to calling him "mon petit monstre." When he asked her to sign a drawing he had done of her, she wrote, "Mais petit-monstre, vous avez fait une horreur! Yvette Guilbert." She was drawn and caricatured by many other artists, some of outstanding skill, but it is Lautrec's presentation of her which became historic, and gave her a place in the long history of the stage. Without Lautrec she would now be forgotten. With him, she lives, a fixed star. By comparison, posters of her by Théophile Steinlen, a grand name in the 1890s, are quite lifeless now.

It was the same story with other female performers. Artists came from all over France, and Europe, to capture images of Loie Fuller, the young dancer from Chicago, who brought her all-electric act to the Folies Bergère theater in the 1890s. She was the first to use electric light to illuminate herself while she danced—standing largely motionless but waving around lacy, pole-backed extensions of her arms in wild flurries. The glaring color effects were completely new and seemed amazing at the time: I calculate that over one thousand artists tried to reproduce the Fuller phenomenon in oil, watercolor, lithographs, and sculpture (I possess a head of her, in alabaster, from 1895). No one quite succeeded in pinning down the movement in art, though Lautrec, with oil sketches on paper, and then a series of lithographs, in fine colors, *au pinceau et au crachis*, came close to it, presenting her as a matte-colored, amorphous, elongated blob, with stubby legs protruding.

In the case of the dancer Jane Avril, just as famous in her day as Guilbert, Lautrec concentrated on her long, thin, black-stockinged legs, with a surrounding aurora of white petticoats. Photographs of her show how remote this was from reality, yet it was also quintessential and, in a sense, true. She was all black-stockinged legs, which she could poise and extend in most extraordinary projection and at unbelievable angles. The artist Grass-Mick did a brilliant drawing of Lautrec sketching her legs at work, and there survive dozens of attempts by Lautrec to get those marvelous legs moving. She was a high-kicker but she also had a trick of getting both arms under her right thigh and moving her leg in a horizontal wiggle at the audience, who loved it. A photograph shows her doing precisely this action, and can be compared to a painting by Lautrec, on brown paper in petrol mixed with oil color, of the same trick. The photo shows that Avril was much prettier than Lautrec would allow, whereas the painting is wonderfully alive with movement and sensuality. Lautrec used the image for one of his most perfect posters, for the Jardin de Paris, in which the dancer and the black-stockinged legs merge into one of the instruments of the orchestra. He also did a poster of her, with flaming orange hair, in a long black dress patterned with a snake around it, which must rank as one of the most striking in the history of advertising. As a reward she went to bed with him, "just once, *comme des amis*." Lautrec became so fond of her he painted her in street clothes, going to and from the theater, with a long sad face and tragic postures: the dark side of the footlights, for she was mentally unstable and ended her life in an asylum for the insane.

Lautrec had the gift, enhanced by persistent hard work, of turning women performers into overwhelming visual personalities. He did this for the *clownesse* Cha-U-Kao, as she was nicknamed (meaning "noisy chaos"), the two English artistes Mary Belfort and May Milton, and the exquisite dancer Marcelle Lender. Lautrec admired Lender very much, especially for the sexual energy she transmitted into her dancing. He did fifteen lithographs of her, one of which, *Marcelle Lender, en buste*, in five colors, is among his finest productions. He also did a magnificent painting of her, *Marcelle Lender dansant le boléro*. When they met, she found him revolting and repulsed his offers of friendship with brutality. He offered her the boléro painting but she refused to take it: "What a horrible man!" This was one of the rare occasions when Lautrec, despite all his efforts, personal and artistic, failed to make any impression on an artiste.

For Lautrec loved women, as tragicomic individuals, and they usually responded, seeing through the degraded, disgusting mask of his face, and the distorted horror of his body, to the human sympathizer and the sensitive artist beneath and behind his deformity. There was often a certain magic between him and women who performed for the public, at a time when many people, certainly most of those who came from Lautrec's background of wealth and quarterings, regarded actresses and music hall stars with the same social contempt they bestowed on demimondaines—only one fragile step above prostitutes.

Hence it is not surprising—natural, rather—that Lautrec, the insider by birth, but the outsider by bodily deformity, should find himself comfortable with the female performers outside society. They might perform with their bodies on stage, or with their bodies in the rooms of brothels and prostitutes' bed-sitting-rooms. But equally, they were engaged in trading their looks, and youth and physical skills for cash. Lautrec thus looked at the female trade in flesh with the eyes of the insider. He made himself at home in certain Paris brothels, where he was welcome as an observer without contempt or hypocrisy, as an inmate indeed in deprivation and suffering. Dégas, also, painted many brothel scenes, not indeed with any hostility. But there is a hard edge to his presentation of whores, an absence of pity or fellow-feeling. Lautrec, by contrast, shows a softer side. When drawing or presenting stage performers, like Avril or Guilbert or even La Goulue, he had to concentrate on turning them into archetypes of themselves, bringing out the touch of caricature which made his depiction of them instantly recognizable. This forbade instinctive tenderness. With whores, however, he did not need to rein in his instincts. The compassion, yielding place only to the fundamental artistic truth, is allowed to flow. It is a fact, and in a way the most interesting fact about Lautrec as the artist of *la comédie humaine*, that his brothel scenes show more pure feeling than anything else he did. These creatures, to most people degraded and soiled, are shown as women, who feel (for instance) lining up for the weekly medical inspection of their intimate parts, as unpleasant as any lady with a *particule* to her name would, in similar circumstances. Lautrec's painting of this dreadful regular ritual is one of his most effectively moving.

He also succeeded in presenting, with truth and tenderness, the affection between women which was characteristic of brothel life at the time. To call it lesbianism is not quite right. It was more a comment on, and a refuge from, the simulated love for men the women were obliged by their trade to produce during working hours. Lautrec, the observer privileged by his ugliness and deformity, to witness scenes denied to all other men, showed this strange force of affection with a sympathy he could not bring to any other kind of human love. It almost at times hovers on the brink of sentimentality, though never tumbling over it. Those who bring to the examination of such works the spirit of prurience miss their quality entirely. They show Lautrec at his best, with his bodily failings giving him powerful advantages for once.

On this point it is worth noting that Lautrec's deformities never prevented him from creating his artistic visions, on paper or on canvas. He held pencil or pen, chalk or brush as firmly and delicately as any other artist. His eyes missed nothing. What his short stature, and the trouble with his legs, did oblige him to do was to sit up close, or stand close, to his canvas when painting. Various photographs show how close he normally positioned himself. (His German contemporary Adolf Menzel, who though not crippled was less than five feet high, did the same.) This meant that Lautrec was never tempted to produce the Impressionist fuzz which ruined the work of so many other painters at that time, Monet not least. In fact Lautrec, like Dégas, Mary Cassat, and others, was never an Impressionist in any real sense. He was a realist, and his deformities strengthened his realistic approach to art, in many ways.

Lautrec was only thirty-six when he died, and it is important to remember he was essentially a young man when his best work was done. But from his early thirties his health began to deteriorate, possibly as a result of syphilis, certainly in consequence of his increasingly heavy drinking. At one time he had to be placed in a clinic for alcoholics, afflicted with insanity. He suffered from delusions and, at times, from delirium tremens (DTs). His decline is described in great detail in Julia Frey's magnificent biography, first published in London in 1994, which draws on over one thousand unpublished letters and other documents hitherto inaccessible. Lautrec's last years were sad, particularly after he ceased to paint. The one redeeming feature was the devotion of his mother, Adele, Comtesse de Toulouse-Lautrec, whom he faithfully portrayed many times. Some other members of his family were hostile. The head of it, his uncle, objected fiercely to Lautrec's brothel paintings, particularly when Lautrec foolishly stored some of them in his castle. Uncle Charles de Toulouse-Lautrec invited

the entire village to witness the destruction of eight of them,
which he burned in front of a gawking butcher and an up-
holsterer, saying, "Now this rubbish will no longer dishonor
my house." He was further incensed when Lautrec insisted on
treating the auto-da-fé as a joke, adding however that he and
Uncle Charles would henceforth have only "funeral relations."
During his decline, a great many of his canvases and works on
paper disappeared and were presumably destroyed. No matter.
Enough has survived to show him to have been a great artist,
a master of the human comedy, who saw life honestly in all
its garish oddity, and steadily enough to paint it accurately.
I find myself, as I grow older, more and more attached to his
work, more inclined not only to admire and take pleasure
in his skill, and daring, and innovation—particularly in his
color combinations—but to laugh with him in his wonder at
humanity and himself.

# CHAPTER SEVEN

# G. K. CHESTERTON: A LIVING, TALKING GARGOYLE

I T I S H A R D to think of Gilbert Keith Chesterton (1874–1936) without laughing. Or so I find. Now this is odd. For GKC (as I shall call him) thought and believed himself to be, insisted he was, a profoundly serious man. He wrote, "I never in my life said anything merely because I thought it funny; though of course I have an ordinary human vainglory, and may have thought it funny because I had said it." The funny thing about this disavowal, however, is that it occurs in chapter 1 of *Orthodoxy* (1908), GKC's summary of his Christian faith, in which for the first time he felt able to align himself completely alongside the Apostles' Creed, though he did not become a Catholic until 1922. He regarded it as his most

important book. Now what was he doing discussing his sense
of humor at the beginning of his chief theological apologia?

The answer is that GKC never regarded humor as inap-
propriate, intrusive, or out of place. On the contrary. It was,
or should be, welcome always and everywhere, especially in
religious discussions. He believed Christianity, properly understood, to be the last haven of secret jokes. It was the smile on
the face of a tortured world. In presenting it he always stressed
its humanity, its *comédie humaine*. Its most important symbol
was the gargoyle, which he called the emblem of Christian ex-
hilaration and generosity, as opposed to the meanness of spirit
of the secularists. He referred to the "lustiness and virile laughter" of the Middle Ages, and he wrote

> Christianity is itself so jolly a thing that it fills the pos-
> sessor of it with a certain jolly exuberance, which sad and
> high-minded rationalists might reasonably mistake for
> buffoonery and blasphemy, just as their prototypes, the
> sad-minded stoics of Rome, did mistake the Christian
> joyousness for buffoonery and blasphemy. The difference
> holds good everywhere, in the cold pagan architecture and
> the grinning gargoyles of Christendom, in the preposter-
> ous motley of the Middle Ages and the dingy dress of
> this rationalist century.

GKC was born in 1874, the same year as Winston Churchill
and Chaim Weizmann. It was a good vintage, which also included celebrated "moderns" such as Gertrude Stein, Robert

Frost, Arnold Schoenberg, and Gustav Holst. But GKC and
Churchill were the only two who combined a deadly serious
purpose with an outstanding sense of humor, liable to burst out
at all times. They also shared an unmistakably jovial appearance and delighted the cartoonists, though each had, when
required, a tremendously sober face, Churchill's expressing a
dogged determination to defend Western civilization, GKC's
a growly transcendental faith in the Christianity he believed to
be that civilization's essence.

Both were fortunate, in my view, that they escaped university, and so were able to develop their individual personalities
without Oxbridge inhibitions and affectation. They were open
to the accusation that they "never really grew up," retaining a
boyish bounce to the end. There, I think, the comparison has
to end, for Churchill was an activist and pragmatist, always
anxious to do things, whereas GKC was always liable to lock
himself into his imagination and idealism. He was "born to
believe." He came from the West London upper-middle classes,
was born and grew up in the Campden Hill area, attended
St. Paul's School—a famous London institution, founded by
John Colet, Erasmus's teacher, in the early sixteenth century—
and surveyed the world as "the Napoleon of Notting Hill." His
father ran a well-known firm of estate agents, which still bears
his name and flourishes. But he gave his children an affection-
ate and literary education dominated by cardboard theaters and
doll actors. (Churchill, by contrast, had two thousand lead soldiers, organized as an infantry division and a cavalry brigade.)
At St. Paul's, that industrious and solemn academy, GKC was

a tall scarecrow, two years behind the others academically, drawing all over his textbooks. So, instead of Oxford, he was sent to the Slade School of Fine Art, where he does not seem to have learned much, and to attend English literature classes at University College, London, where he read a lot. He continued to draw, though he never made his living by it, and instead became a freelance journalist and writer, extending his range to include lecturing and speaking in public debates.

Until marriage, his home was essentially the pubs and wine bars of Fleet Street. He gradually filled out, ceasing to be a scarecrow and becoming an immense gargoyle of his own manufacture, composed of beer and wine (not spirits) and sandwiches eaten in odd moments. He was never a drunk—far from it—but he celebrated drinking. He wrote, in his essay "The Wine When it is Red," "No animal ever invented anything so bad as drunkenness—or so good as drink." An easygoing, swift, and prolific composer of verse, and occasionally of high-quality poetry, he wrote many drinking songs, and one of his best poems, "The Rolling English Road," begins

Before the Romans came to Rye or out to Severn strode,
The rolling English drunkard made the rolling English
    road.
A reeling road, a rolling road that rambles round the shire,
And after him the parson ran, the sexton and the squire;
A merry road, a mazy road, and such as we did tread
The night we went to Birmingham by way of Beachy Head.

GKC might have become an aimless bohemian and petered out, wasting his intellectual coin in endless pub conversation, as so many did and do. He was saved by marriage, his wife, Frances, being a sensible and practical person. When he got married, he turned up at St. Mary Abbotts, the imposing Victorian parish church of Kensington, for the ceremony correctly garbed in a morning coat, smart waistcoat, and striped pants. But he forgot to put on a tie. One was hurriedly bought at a nearby shop. When he knelt at the altar, the labels on the soles of his new shoes were plainly visible, and caused titters in the congregation. The best man had the married couple's luggage safely delivered to the station, but GKC missed the train. One of his sayings was: "To love anything is to see it at once under lowering clouds of danger." Marriage to Frances brought out such a burst of affection that he went straight from the ceremony, without telling anyone, to a gunsmith to buy a revolver and bullets "with which to defend my new wife." The couple eventually arrived at their honeymoon hotel but he went out for a walk and got hopelessly lost. That set a pattern, especially when GKC undertook speaking engagements all over the country, traveling to them, and from them, alone. He never seems to have kept a diary, and one of the most famous tales told about him is that Frances received a cable from him stating simply "Am in Market Harborough. Where should I be?"

The Chestertons remained an intensely close couple until his death in 1936. But they never had children. The word went around about GKC, whose obvious happiness was much envied by the intelligentsia, that the marriage was never consummated. This rumor was strenuously denied by Maisie Ward, who wrote the best biography of GKC and had exceptional opportunities to discover all the truth about him. She was able to reveal that Frances had repeatedly sought medical advice about childbearing. But the rumors persisted. It is a curious fact that the genial GKC, who bore malice to none, and rejoiced in countless loving friends, was regarded with rancor by some who never met him, particularly academics. They resented and envied his enjoyment in his faith. His childlessness, a source of great sorrow to him and his wife, was used to snipe at the basis of their marriage, in exactly the same way it was used against Thomas and Jane Welsh Carlyle. The hostility to GKC persists in British academia (not in American colleges, fortunately), where the strong atheist and secular puritan elements have successfully kept his work off the curricula in schools and universities, thereby depriving children and students of much innocent enjoyment.

If GKC was ever aware that his abundant enjoyment of life and writing aroused jealousy, he never let on. He was too busy. All his working life, from the Slade to his death, he was tremendously productive. His output was enormous and covered a spectacular variety of topics. He produced the best book on Robert Browning ever written, and one on Dickens that became an immediate classic. His lives of St. Francis and St. Thomas Aquinas are miracles of intuition, if not of scholarship. No man ever worked harder to convey truth and, at the

same time, to avoid acquiring and transmitting facts. All four
of these books are a joy to read, and radically increase the joy
we find in exploring the work of their subjects. Of course,
Browning, Dickens, and St. Francis all loved jokes, but "no
one ever got a laugh out of the *Summa theologica* before." GKC
published many other books, often collections of his essays
and articles. There were literally thousands of these. A large
proportion appeared in defense of Christianity and, later, of
Catholicism. They were often delivered in spoken form as
well, in debates with skeptics and atheists. It was the grand age
of public debate, before it was undermined first by wireless,
then by TV. The religious and antireligious controversialists
were particularly active. Their productivity was staggering.
GKC must have written or spoken over ten million words
about God and Christianity. George Bernard Shaw, in addition to his plays, poured out articles, speeches, pamphlets,
and manifestos. H. G. Wells produced similar ephemera in
vast quantities, plus his novels, and his huge *Outline of History*, which GKC greatly admired but also trounced, a typical
Chesterton paradox. Robert Blatchford, GKC's principal opponent in print, wrote millions of words savaging Christianity,
then ended up a spiritualist, poor fellow. Another of GKC's
opponents, Joseph McCabe, a Franciscan friar who unfrocked
himself and became an apostle of atheism and scourge of the
church, wrote over two hundred books and pamphlets, and
translated another fifty scientific and free-thinking works, including *The Riddle of the Universe* by Ernst Haeckel, a forma-
tive influence on Nazi race theory.

Thanks largely to GKC and Shaw, both kindly and good-natured men, these public debates and print wars were usually even tempered and courteous. Shaw wrote of GKC's treatment of him, "Nothing could have been more generous." GKC reciprocated: "I have never read a reply to me by Bernard Shaw which did not leave me in a better and not a worse temper, and which did not seem to come out of inexhaustible fantasies of fair-mindedness and intellectual geniality. . . . I am proud of him as a foe even more than as a friend." Of course the two men shared a sense of humor of infinite richness and resilience, based upon a shared belief that everything was fair subject matter for jokes—Shaw's Fabian socialism no less than GKC's Christianity. Both also took the view that politics and religion were not to be made private, personal, and secretive, but were properly proclaimed from the rooftops. "Shout it out!" as Shaw put it, GKC adding, "A man can no more possess a private religion than he can possess a private sun and moon."

GKC's wit, and his jokes, were often based upon paradox, and the inversion of familiar truth. He was a total individualist, seeing everything, as if for the first time in history, with his own eyes, and nobody else's. To understand him it is often helpful not only to repeat what he said, which made others laugh, but to cite what made him laugh. He long forestalled Foucault, for instance, in upending the relative positions of the sane and insane. In *Orthodoxy*, he wrote, "The madman is not the man who has lost his reason. The madman is the man who has lost everything except his reason." His favorite asylum joke went thus: "In the ward, a man was just leaving, cured, when he suddenly gave the matron a tremendous kick on her bottom. Upbraided, he said: 'God clearly ordained me to do it.' At that point, an old man with a white beard, standing nearby, interjected: 'You are a liar. I never gave any such command.'"

GKC felt that the sharp line dividing sane and insane into white and black was misconceived. To him, reason was neutral, morally, and rationalism was suspect, more so than "dottiness," a favorite word of his. In *Heretics*, he wrote, "Happiness is a mystery, like religion, and should never be rationalised." He liked to quote Thomas Carlyle, "Men are mostly fools," and add, "Christianity, with a surer and more reverend realism, says that they are all fools." But then, to him, a fool was another name for a jester, and he liked to think that Christianity brought out the jester in man—and woman. He admitted that most of his own jokes were aimed at men who, at any rate before the First World War, when he learned his craft as a public speaker, were overwhelmingly masculine. He said, "It is easier to make a man laugh at a bad joke, but more worthwhile to get a woman to laugh at a good joke." He did not fight the sex war, which would have been an abomination to him, had he understood the concept. But he noted there were differences between the sexes: "A male friend likes him, and leaves him as he is. His wife loves him and is always trying to turn him into somebody else." Frances certainly failed to turn GKC into somebody else—a businesslike, appointment-keeping, meticulous, and tidy person, always in the right place at the right time, in the right clothes—though she tried. But she did

change his appearance, if only superficially. She decided to
put him inside a voluminous, all-concealing cloak, crowned
by a wide, black, sombrero-like felt hat. This he accepted, as
convenient and comfortable, and wore forever after. It gave
him an instantly recognizable silhouette and made him one of
the best-known shapes in the country. But GKC never spoke
about Frances's attempts to re-form him. His relationship with
her was hallowed ground. To some extent, all women were hallowed. He never made a joke against the female sex, as such,
because to GKC the act of making a joke was one of the most
serious decisions you could possibly make, on a par with publishing a political manifesto, or a declaration of war. But he
liked to laugh at such jokes, especially if they involved verbal
sleight of hand. Thus he quoted the case of Moll Cresswell, a
famous seventeenth-century procuress, who left in her will £10
to have a panegyric preached at her funeral. A clergyman was
found to do this admirably. He preached on morality, and said
of the deceased, "She was born well, she lived well and died
well. For she was born a Creswell, she lived in Clerkenwell,
and she died in Bridewell [a notorious women's prison]." He
also quoted (or invented) a letter a conscientious man wrote
to the Home Office: "Dear Sir, I enclose a cheque for one
pound in payment of a dog license. It is true I have no dog.
It is also true I never had a dog. But I have a wife who is such
a b— that I feel in conscience obliged to accept the financial
responsibility of ownership. Yours faithfully."

GKC saw divorce as a more terrible thing than all the alternative remedies for an unhappy marriage, though he said,

"What do I know of the problem? I have always been happily married." As one who longed in vain for a child, he regarded abortion with peculiar horror. When questioned about it on the platform, he used to quote a case (supplied to him, I think, by Maurice Baring), in which one doctor consulted another about the termination of a pregnancy: "The father was syphilitic. The mother had TB. Of the children already born, the first was blind, the second died of weakness, the third was deaf and dumb, the fourth tuberculous. The woman was now pregnant again. What would you have done?" "I would have terminated the pregnancy." "Then you would have murdered Beethoven."

GKC was similarly opposed to any form of playing God with life. Euthanasia was for him a usurpation of the Divine Right. He loathed a way of thinking just coming into vogue in his day: "social engineering." The idea of shoveling human beings around as though they were quantities of concrete was an abomination. Equally he flatly refused to have anything to do with eugenics, the fashionable cure-all for the health of an expanding population, which was vociferously supported by most of the leading British and American intellectuals between the wars, notably Shaw and Wells. They both favored the painless dispatch of the insane (in certain circumstances) and stringent control of "the right to breed." GKC lumped euthanasia, abortion, birth control, and eugenics all together as "the philosophy of Death." Of course he wrote and debated these issues, on both sides of the Atlantic, before the full horrors of social engineering were practiced in Hitler's "final solution," and Stalin's Gulag archipelago. But he rightly predicted that the twentieth century would be a leaden age of mass killing by the totalitarian state, and most of his warnings were fully vindicated by events shortly after his death.

GKC never sought to be a politician, "as it is more desirable to amuse people directly, and of set purpose, than by accident." He disliked "isms" and "movements." He wrote in 1923, "The meanest man is immortal and the mightiest movement is temporal, not to say temporary." He backed schemes to make small portions of land or other property available to all, but refused to use the word "distributist." For many years he ran a periodical, called *GK's Weekly*, setting forth the views of himself and like-minded people on a huge range of issues. He never claimed he was able, or wanted, to make people affluent, not least because he was always suspicious of the rich. He never spared the privileged few. "Honour is a luxury for aristocrats but it is a necessity for hall-porters." "Science has many uses. Its chief one, however, is to provide long words to cover the errors of the rich: 'Kleptomania' for example." "The British oligarch does not rest, as so many oligarchies do, on the cruelty of the rich to the poor. Or even on the kindness of the rich to the poor. It rests on the perennial and unfailing kindness of the poor to the rich." "To be clever enough to get all that money, you must be stupid enough to want it." "Gold in banks is unreality. But coins in your pocket are a kind of truth." And: "The man who does not look at his change is no true poet."

This last reminds us that GKC was a man perpetually striving to sum up essential knowledge in simple remarks. He loved the one-liner, particularly if it encompassed a joke, because then it was more likely to be remembered. He wrote detective stories around the character of an old priest who was fertile in such observations. Father Brown says, "An artist will betray himself by some sort of sincerity." And: "Every work of art has one indispensable merit: the centre of it is simple, however much the circumference may be complicated." And: "Where does a wise man kick a pebble? On the beach. Where does a wise man kick a leaf? In the forest." "If you convey to a woman that something ought to be done, there is always a dreadful danger that she will suddenly do it."

GKC passed his life in trying to make his readers think for themselves by giving little tugs of the leash with which he held them to his writings. He was not a great poet. But he was a man who, once or twice, wrote a great poem, as I discovered at the age of fourteen, when I learned by heart, for an elocution competition, his poem "Lepanto," a wonderful fireworks display of burning faith decorated by knowledge worn gently. But in a sense his life was a poem, translating the thoughts of a big, plump, ungainly, and blundering man into things of sweetness and enlightenment. He wrote, "To be born into this world is to be born into uncongenial surroundings, hence to be born into a romance." But he was always insisting that his romantic view of things was the true realism. He wrote, "Reason is itself a matter of faith. It is an act of faith to assert that our thoughts have any relation to reality at all." That is why, he added, "poets do not go mad—but chess-players do." A human always searches for profundity, but "Angels can fly because they take themselves lightly." It is right to be humble. "But everyman is worthy of the best." In his book on Charles Dickens, he wrote, "There is a great man who makes every man feel small. But the really great man is the man who makes every man feel great." It might be said of him that he tried to be a practical man, but poetry was always breaking in: "A third-class carriage is a community. But a first-class carriage is a place of wild hermits." His final thought on religion was a paradoxical blend of pessimism and optimism: "The Christian ideal has not been tried and found wanting. It has been found difficult and left untried." He accompanied his observations by one of his rare pieces of introspection: "It is a fine thing to forgive your enemies. But it is a finer thing not to be too eager to forgive yourself." GKC never sought to deny the awful difficulty of life and things. In one of his best poems, "The Ballad of the White Horse," he wrote:

I tell you nought for your comfort,
Yea, nought for your desire,
Save that the sky grows darker yet
And the sea rises higher.

But in another fine poem, "The Secret People," he imagined a great race of ordinary persons, strong in their collective wisdom, who might yet speak out to rebuke the great powers of the world, who have made such a mess of it.

We are the people of England; and we have not spoken
   yet.
Smile at us, pay us, pass us. But do not quite forget.

He died without speaking any famous last words. Had he
done so, they would have constituted a warning, enshrined
in a jest. In a sense he had already spoken them once, when
ill: "Lying in bed would be an altogether perfect and supreme
experience if only one had a coloured pencil long enough to
draw on the ceiling."

# CHAPTER EIGHT

# DAMON RUNYON: GUYS, DOLLS, AND THE PUPPET MASTER

T HERE ARE CERTAIN humorists who become cult figures. Their admirers regard them as geniuses. Others are not so sure. There is no arguing the point. In Britain this position was occupied in the twentieth century by Pelham Grenville Wodehouse (1881–1975), whom many, led by Evelyn Waugh, proclaimed "the greatest writer of English of the day." In America it was held by (Alfred) Damon Runyon (1880–1946), hailed by Ernest Hemingway as "the master of us all." Both were accomplished stylists, writing in a hieratic they invented, which was peculiar to themselves and inimitable. Both Waugh and Hemingway changed the way people wrote English in fiction, and influenced so many authors as to change the language. Wodehouse and Runyon did not do that: they were eccentric and egregious, creating their own idioms, peculiar grammar, syntax, and punctuation, and making their mannerist prose inseparable from their subject matter. Each created a milieu which never did or could exist, but has a powerful reality of its own, like a fairy tale. The reader-addict can get lost in it, and emerge, blinking, into the light of common day.

Damon Runyon was one year Wodehouse's senior and both lived in the New York area for many years, and their paths crossed, for Wodehouse was involved in Broadway musicals at a time when Runyon covered show business there. Indeed in 1935 Runyon wrote (with Howard Lindsay) a farce, *A Slight Case of Murder*, though it was not until four years after his death that his stories were turned into a hit musical, *Guys and Dolls* (1950). Runyon was a newspaper man all his life, and produced his material first in column form, until its success in book form, beginning with *Guys and Dolls* in 1931, allowed him to retire from regular hackwork. His compilation of tales—*From First to Last, On Broadway, Take it Easy, In Our Town*, and others—constitute a large and homogenous whole, all written in the same manner, about the same people, in the same area, and with the same outlook.

As a form of mannerist writing they are in the highest class, taking rank with Kipling's *Plain Tales from the Hills*, or Somerville and Ross's *Experiences of an Irish RM*, or Jack London's outback stories, or Somerset Maugham's Far East tales, or the Hollywood of Dashiell Hammett and Raymond Chandler. Runyon, unlike Wodehouse, but like Kipling, was essentially a writer of short stories, which could not be fleshed out into novels. But many characters occur repeatedly, and the oeuvre as a whole has a unity.

Runyon is a quintessentially American comic writer. A central theme in this comedy springs from history: the creation of order out of chaos, which was the story of the United States in the eighteenth and nineteenth centuries, and well into the twentieth. In the course of the order-creation, the original chaos is necessary—i.e., in the Mississippi River valley, in the Great Plains and Rockies, and the conquest of the West. Cowboys and Indians, gunslingers and outlaws, hustlers and rustlers, sheriffs and marshals, saloon-bar proprietors and Diamond Lils, all are part of the primeval chaos, until American order emerges, and the tales cease. Runyon's Broadway and Manhattan, with excursions to take in Brooklyn and Queens, St. Louis and Atlantic City, even Chicago and LA (though these are Foreign Parts), are made to seem chaotic. They are composed of gangsters and gamblers, speakeasies, nightclubs, and "joints," and life is punctuated by regular lawbreaking and occasional murders and kidnappings. But these are fairy tales, not reality, so Runyon's Manhattan is essentially an orderly/disorderly place, conforming to rules and limitations, in which an apparent anarchy is actually restrained by large numbers of things which are not done. It is even religious up to a point, with "Father Leonard" and "the Pastor" available to perform marriages and baptisms. Guys have dolls, but people get married rather than live in sin. Babies are sacrosanct, as is shown by the tale "Butch Minds the Baby," Big Butch being a sort of

retired safebreaker. The police, with names like Cassidy and
Callahan, are both corrupt and honest, ruthless and tender-
hearted and sentimental. No one swears, or if they do it is
offstage and the words are not reproduced. This is a pre-four-
letter-word culture in every respect. There is no explicit and
very little implicit sex, and no dirty jokes. Runyon ran his own
Hays Office, which is unobtrusive but absolute. Women usually
emerge on top, which is necessary to preserve morality. The
universe of Runyon's Manhattan has its own Ten Command-
ments springing from a Judeo-Christian background.

Yet the fairy-tale world has a carapace of realism, often
disguised as brutality. Runyon essentially covers the era of
Melting Pot America, between the end of the Civil War and
the Wall Street crash. Manhattan was its popular apotheosis,
absorbing millions of immigrants from all over Europe, as well
as an underclass of Southern Negroes and Asians. Runyon
speaks to them, about them, and, in a sense, for them. That
is the essence of his style. He always writes in the present, for
that was the only tense the immigrants could master, to begin
with. This has the marvelous double effect of giving his tales
melting-pot authenticity and immediacy. There is no past and
no future. All has happened, is happening, and will happen
now, and in the next few minutes. It is a stroke of pure genius,
on Runyon's part, to hit on this dodge, stick to it mercilessly,
and follow its logic with ingenuity.

Runyon enhances his presentist style by judicious punctuation, the use of "furthermore" instead of a period, a clever
use of commas amounting to genius at times, and a sentence-

beginning, "I wish to say," for emphasis. He often ends a sentence with a comma, followed by "indeed" or "at that." These tricks are judiciously spaced out, so they do not annoy. Runyon has a mannerist vocabulary assembled with cunning, part composed of underworld argot, often genuine, part invented. A pele-box is a safe. A stuss-house is a late-night club. Scratch is cash. So is "the old do-re-mi." A deuce is $2. A finnif is $5, also known as "a pound note." A snatch is a kidnap, and to finger is to denote the object of a snatch (or give it away). Girls are dolls, broads, pancakes, cookies, and tomatoes (the last "very vulgar"). To "give everybody a square rattle" is to be fair. To "pig's it" is to renege. Gondola is a foot. Java is coffee. Kisser is face. Smuch is mouth, as in "He kissed her ker-plump right on the smuch." "Shylocks" will lend you money (at high rates) right at the gambling table. A warm squattivoo is the electric chair, usually in Sing Sing. "Corned" is liquored up, and there are many words for alcohol and its consequences, to rival the list of 340 expressions for intoxication compiled by Edmund Wilson in Prohibition America. Thus "this guy gets himself pretty well organized" by "belting the old grape" and so "feeling very brisk."

Among expressions I have noted as choice Runyon are as follows. "Now this is strictly the old ackamarack as the Lemon Drop Kid cannot even spell arthritis, let alone have it." "I have long ago come to the conclusion that all life is six-to-four against" (Sam the Gonoph). "A smart old broad. A pity she is so nefarious." Angie the Ox is "an Importer, including artichokes and extorsion." Nicely-Nicely "dearly loves to commit eating." (When thin, he is Edmund Jones.) He is also known as a "Hooray Henry," a term invented by Runyon (see the story "Lonely Heart"). Scoodles Shea is "a big red-headed muzzler with a lot of freckles and a wide grin all over his kisser." Black Mike is "a guinea." Joe Goss, who runs a nightclub in Atlantic City "just off the Broadwalk," is "a lily for looks."

This brings us to the list of characters, who constitute the particular strength of Runyon as a top mannerist writer. He himself, or his narrator, is never exactly described. But he is characterized: "I am known to one and all as a guy who is just around." He is occasionally pounced on by hoodlums who want his company, for reasons they do not give. At such times, in addition to being cowardly he is frightened that the hoodlum will commit some wrongdoing in which, being in his company, the narrator will be implicated. So: "I am trying to think up some place to go where people will see me, and remember afterwards that I am there, in case it is necessary for them to remember." At other times, a hoodlum spots him in a restaurant, such as Bobby's Chophouse on Broadway, eating Bobby's famous beef stew, and without asking, eats off his plate. The narrator puts up with this, as he puts up with being hoicked off. But as a rule he is a mere observer and recorder, whose ambition is simply to keep out of trouble, while retaining a ringside seat at its enactment.

Of the characters, there are three main types: guys who are gangsters or gamblers, and dolls who cover a variety of activities and nonactivity. It is sometimes difficult to distinguish between gangsters and gamblers. Indeed many hoodlums also gamble. The gangsters include three "notorious hoodlums from Brooklyn," Harry the Horse, Little Isadore, and Spanish John. There is Rusty Charlie, a redhead, who also has a red-haired wife. Milk Ear Willie and Hymie Banjo Eyes speak for themselves. Horse Thief is also known as Horsey. Gloomy Gus Smallwood also speaks for himself, but is "written out of the script" or, as Runyon puts it, "guzzled in Philly" (murdered in Philadelphia). Jew Louie is not exactly a gangster, being a "Shylock," but requires protection and strong-armers to ensure his victims pay the high interest they owe. Then there are hoodlums described as "seen at Detroit's." Detroit holds high-stakes craps games, illegally of course, and among those "seen at" his place are Sleepout Sam Levinsky, Lone Louie (from Harlem), and three men described as "high shot gangsters," Nick the Greek, Grey John, and Okay Okun. There is a category of gangsters who are exceptionally strong and tough, known as a gorill. Rusty Charlie is one, Earthquake another. Knife O'Halloran speaks for himself. So does the Seldom Seen Kid. Red Henry, "who does not take a bath since he is out of Dannemora" (a Federal penitentiary), but who is nevertheless known to dance with the rich Harriet MacKyle, is another gorill. Other gangsters include three noted as attending a big Broadway wedding described by Runyon. These are Skeets Boliver, Tony Bertazzola, and Rochester Red. Gangsters fall into three main racial categories, Italian, Jews, and Irish, but there are a few blacks ("from Harlem"), Spanish-speaking Puerto Ricans or Cubans, and indeterminates. In the story "Dark Dolores" we hear of the three St. Louis gangs who hold a peace conference in neutral Atlantic City, brokered by Black Mike Marrio.

The gamblers include Educated Edmund, who plays klob; Regret the Horse Player; Big Nig, who runs the crap school; Olive Street Oscar, described simply as "a betting man"; Dave the Dude, another all-rounder; Hot Horse Herbie, a tipster with "a depressing kisser"; and Jack the Beefer, "a gambler's nark." The Sky, as you'd expect, is a high roller; Brandy Bottle Bates "has a large beezer and a head like a pear"; and Meyer Marmalade bets on football. What Frying Pan Joe does can be left to the imagination. The bookmakers include Bookie Bob and Willie the Worrier. The Brain is an amorphous or protean character who hovers over both gambling and crime. His real name is Arnold Rosenthal, and his cunning annoys people, so that Homer Swing hires Daffy Jack to stick a knife into him.

The dolls are endless. Lovely Lou works in the 300 Club, owned by Miss Missouri Martin. Maud Milligan is Big Nig's doll, and Big Marge is Goodtime Charlie's doll. Princess O'Hara is the daughter of King O'Hara, who drives a hackney coach. One of the most notable of the dolls is Lola Sapola, who comes from a circus family known as The Rolling Sapolas. She is variously described as "A doll about five feet high and five feet wide" and "The Wide Doll." Runyon says: "She looks all hammered down. Her face is as wide as her shoulders and makes me think of a full moon." Among other actions ascribed to her is to "slam Dave the Dude in his solar plexus." Amelia Bodkin is the doll of Jabez Tuesday, described as "the rich millionaire." Hortense Hathaway is the daughter of Skush O'Brien, the cab driver.

Drivers and the like are often important in the stories. David the Dude's driver is Wojo Joe. Solid John, also known as Dobber, is the doorman at Detroit's, and the Stick Guy there is Scranton Slim. The doorman at the Woodcock Inn is Slugsy Sachs. At the 300 Club the doorman is Soldier Sweeney. These people humanize the background and often work the machinery of Runyon's plots. Other regular inhabitants and linkmen are Judge Goldfobber, Doc Bodecker, and the Widow Crumb. There are various journalists or "newsscribes," such as Ambrose Hammer, and Waldo Winchester, supposedly based on Walter Winchell. Marvin Clay represents café society, the actor Paul Hawley the stage, and Buddy Donaldson the songwriting profession. The most notable of the musicians is Walter Gumple the trombonist, based upon Paul Whiteman the bandleader. These characters serve to give the world of Runyon authenticity and place it in a definite historical context.

But beyond a certain point, Runyon is not aiming at authenticity or historical truth. His object is consistency to his own creation, and its poetic truth. You can live in his Broadway world, but you cannot find it in reality. It is not true but in Runyon's imagination. It has no more physical connection with the actual Manhattan of the twenties than the Thames does with the world that Kenneth Grahame, a contemporary of Runyon, describes in *The Wind in the Willows*. That is its strength as a work of art. It never gets out of date because it never was *in* date. The story "Sense of Humor" describes a practical joker named Hot Foot who goes around Broadway looking for preoccupied individuals into whose shoe soles he can stick, unobserved, a lighted match. It is called "giving them a hot foot." Nothing more is known about him, or what he did before he became addicted to this annoying habit, or what became of him after he was too easily recognizable to get away with it anymore. He lives in an instant of time, and that is all which is required of him, for the purposes of Runyon's art. In enjoying Runyon's stories there has to be, in Coleridge's words, "a willing suspension of disbelief," and once this is conceded, the magic works. Indeed, Runyon's Manhattan is a magic isle, full of strange sounds which give delight and hurt not. When Runyon pulls down the curtain, and we close the book, the characters, "all spirits, are melted into air, into thin air." The concrete canyons of New York, the brightly lit theaters of Broadway, Mindy's Restaurant, the 300 Club, Detroit's, and the Woodcock Inn "dissolve and like this insubstantial pageant faded, leave not a wrack behind." Runyon's guys and dolls "are such stuff as dreams are made on," and their "little life is rounded with a sleep." But while on the page still, they are "very lively, indeed."

# CHAPTER NINE

# W. C. FIELDS: THE DONG WITH THE LUMINOUS NOSE

W. C. FIELDS, OR more properly William Claude Dukenfield, was the quintessential American comedian. He came from the background created by the freak master Phineas T. Barnum, from 1830, with his Dime Museum, featuring a mermaid; General Tom Thumb and his midget wife, Lavinia Warren; and Washington's nurse, Joice Heth, a black woman reputedly 160 years old. Born in 1880, he started as a juggler in such shows, graduated into burlesque and then vaudeville (1898–1915), worked with the Ziegfeld Follies on the stage (1915–1930), made a dozen silent movies (1915–1928), and then thirty-two talkies (1930–1944), before dying in 1946.

Reconstructing Fields's life and career is a messy business, for he was prone to monstrous exaggerations about himself, buttressed by downright lies. Most books about him are unreliable, including his "official biography" by Blythe Foote Fink. However, the best of the Hollywood star–historians, Simon Louvish, has done a good job, in his *The Man on the Flying Trapeze: The Life and Times of W .C. Fields* (1997). Most of the lies have been identified, the exaggerations toned down, and the truth dredged out. His movies survive, apart from four missing silent shorts. So do some radio tapes on the Charlie McCarthy puppet show, 1933–1943, and there are the texts of sketches written by himself: sixteen in the Library of Congress and eighteen in the Fowler/Walker Collection. Some thirty-two other sketches are missing. Among the highlights of Fields's career was his appearance (beating out Charles Laughton for the part) as Mr. Micawber in David Selznick's 1935 MGM movie of *David Copperfield*, with Freddie Bartholomew, Basil Rathbone, Lionel Barrymore, Elsa Lanchester, and Roland Young as Heep. Fields was proud of having made this classic Dickens adaptation, perhaps the best ever. His only complaint was that "It didn't include a poo-room scene." The director, George Cukor, said Fields was "perfect" and his scenes were completed in a mere ten days. The other highlight was his 1940 movie *My Little Chickadee* with Mae West, in which each wrote their own parts. However, Louvish argues, and many agree with him, that Fields's best show was his 1935 movie *Man on the Flying Trapeze*.

Readers can judge for themselves, for most of the oeuvre

is easy to get ahold of nowadays. But in my view, his master-piece was W. C. Fields, the man and the actor, on or off stage and screen, a part he created and added to throughout his life: angry and irascible (not the same thing), witty and bawdy, lustful and mean, suspicious and obsessive, indeed paranoid, full of hates and feuds, xenophobic, racist, misogynist, and with every healthy and unhealthy prejudice known to man. As his own scriptwriter, there was no essential difference between the man and his parts, all of which were similar and did not change over the years.

His father was an immigrant from Yorkshire, who retained his accent to his dying day. I can detect Yorkshire tones in Fields's own speech, and certainly in his character. His mother was of German origin, and "that figures, too," as Mae West said. The place of birth was Philadelphia, then a highly reli-gious, wide-open city, with seven hundred churches and three hundred brothels. Fields's fair-barker tone was equally well adapted for preaching from a pulpit and for drumming up trade in a red-light area. His fondness for his birthplace was part of his act. In *My Little Chickadee*, about to be lynched as the Masked Bandit, he was asked, "Any last words?" "Yes, I'd like to see Paris before I die. Philadelphia will do!" He is said to be buried under a tombstone carved "I'd rather be in Philadelphia." But the truth is his ashes are in a casket marked simply "W. C. Fields, 1880–1946."

Fields called himself "Philadelphia's most distinguished va-grant since Franklin." He claimed he quarreled with his father, left school, and went into showbiz at eleven. In fact he worked in a cigar store and as a "cash boy" in a department store before becoming a juggler, aged sixteen. He began as "the tramp juggler" and dressed as a tramp for five years. He said, "I don't believe Mozart, Liszt, Paderewski, or Kreisler worked any harder than I did." He also said, "A comedian is best when he is hungry." His role was "The Comic Juggler," which included getting laughs at his incompetence. He also did "The Lazy Juggler." His act involved large numbers of cigar boxes, billiard balls, and cues (balancing two balls on the end of a cue), and tricks involving throwing a lighted cigar into the air and catching it in his mouth. There was also "an umbrella caper." His act gradually expanded to take in a pool table and a series of tricks performed thereon. It was organic. Indeed most of his physical jokes, on stage or screen, were variations or expansions of his original pool table performance, but involving cars, bathrooms, barber's chairs, yachts, and golf courses. His pool and golf tricks went through countless transformations.

At what point drink entered his act and life is not clear. In his early stage career he performed "Olio Acts," tricks in front of the oilcloth stage curtain lowered for scene changing. The chorus was known as the Monte Carlo Girls, and he married one of them, Harriet "Hattie" Hughes, later a worthy opponent in a spectacular marital war. According to Blythe Foote Fink, he did not drink before marriage but, soon after, took to sipping weak brandy and ginger ale. Then "graduated to Scotch whiskey, to Irish Whisky to Bourbon to martinis." Liquor inspired his only poem, "A Drink with Something in It":

There is something about a martini
A tingle remarkably pleasant
A yellow, a mellow-martini
I wish I had one at present.
There is something about an Old Fashioned
That kindles a cardiac glow
It's soothing and soft and impassioned
As a lyric by Swinburne or Poe.

In 1938 Fields said he had calculated that he had drunk $185,000 worth of whiskey in forty-two years. After Joe Louis knocked out Schmeling, the super-fit German champion, Fields said, "It simply bears out what I have always contended. A kidney needs a good alcoholic lining to stand up under wear and tear. Schmeling was the victim of clean living. If Louis or any other professional slasher dealt me such a blow their hands would crumple from the impact. As a result of long and serious drinking, I've developed ripples of muscles over my kidneys. I will live to be one hundred and twelve years old and perhaps a fortnight longer than that, and I deserve it because I've gone out of my way to live the wrong way. Some of my best friends are bartenders, but most of them die young. They can dish it out but they can't take it."

Fields's self-presentation as an accomplished drinking man, a genius of alcoholic consumption, was an addition to his on-stage, real-life character, which went with formal suits, cravats, gray top hat, and silver-topped cane. He liked to wear spats.

Drinking did not impair his work. He was never drunk on stage or on the set. On the contrary he was celebrated as a hard and highly efficient worker, a "good study" who always knew his lines, and a money saver for the studios. At various times in the thirties, he earned more cash in a year than any other male star.

He looked like a drinker, though. Rosy cheeks, red ears and neck, Ascot gray topper at an angle, screwed-up eyes, double chins, and, above all, the Nose. His skin was fair and prone to eczema and blotches. At some time he may have had an operation to remove the cartilage in his nose, leaving it soft and pulpy. He may also have suffered from a nose condition known as rosacea. Or he may have shared a complaint with J. Pierpont Morgan called rhinophyma. His nose became his most prominent feature and a source of jokes, his most valuable stock-in-trade. He said it was worth "fifty thousand bucks" to him.

The nose, the furrowed frown, the pursed, tight mouth, the unrelenting eyes, and biting tongue went into the permanent Fields character. He radiated irascibility and invincible dislikes. As an eight-year-old paper delivery boy he had been attacked by savage house dogs, and he hated the canine species thereafter. The text of a soliloquy was found in 1971 entitled "Why Alcohol has taken the place of the dog as Man's Best Friend." Extracts include "Alcohol can take care of itself, which is more than a dog can do. . . . Whiskey doesn't need to be periodically wormed, it does not need to be fed or trained. You never have to train a bottle of grog. A dog will run up and lick your hand. No bottle will do that. If the whiskey starts licking your hand, I advise you to leave off for a while. Say ten minutes." Even so, Fields used dogs. He made a silent short, *Fido the Beautiful Dog*. There is also a sketch, "Buster the Dog," in *It's a Gift*. He is believed to have possessed dogs in the 1920s, and owned them in the late 1930s too. But these were guard dogs, essential to a suspicious man who kept large quantities of valuable liquor on his premises. He never had a dog in his scripts by preference. What he liked as material for joke sketches were golf, tennis, railroad stations and saloons, cars, yachts, doctors' and dentists' surgeries (especially injections), hats, and anything to do with water. He liked ropes too—Mae West shoots the rope off his neck in the *Little Chickadee* hanging scene. One reason he liked Will Rogers (other friends were Eddie Cantor and Bert Williams, "the Lucky Coon") was that he was one-quarter Cherokee, "a wizard with a rope," and "World Champion Lasso Manipulator." But Fields disliked Rogers's lack of hate: Rogers: "I never met a man I didn't like." Fields: "I never met a dog or a baby I didn't hate." He manufactured hate jokes: "What are you, Chinese peoples?" "Who's the head myeroon round here?" "Don't vote for Franklin Disraeli Roosevelt." "Is he a full-blooded Indian?" "Not the way I play it." "I understand you buried your wife recently." "Had to—she died." "So you never drink water?" "No. Fish f—k in it." "Women are like elephants. I like to look at them but I don't want to own one." "Sleep is the most beautiful experience in life—except drink." He coined jokes but used old ones. "As for the war, I'm ready to take up arms at a moment's notice. The legs can follow later." "Why is a cat's tail like a long journey?" "Because it has fur to go." (Alternatively: "So fur to the end.")

Fields had a particular hatred for the Internal Revenue Service, which he was convinced was anxious to ruin him and send him to jail. He said he had over seven hundred different bank accounts, to fox them. He liked to have large amounts of cash in easy reach: a lump of high-value bills was kept in one pocket of his dressing gown. The other held thirty-six keys to strong rooms and other safe places where he kept liquor. He was not anti all officials. He was on good terms with J. Edgar Hoover, head of the FBI, with whom he shared many hatreds, especially of Eleanor Roosevelt. They met over an obscene cartoon of her which, held upside down, showed her vagina. Hoover wrote to him, "It means so much to me to know that the Bureau can call on loyal friends like you in time of need."

The great event in Fields's life which changed and prolonged his showbiz career was the discovery that he was a master of speech as well as manipulative comedy. In his juggling career he was totally silent; he made a virtue of it. His pool room and golfing acts, which launched first his stage, then his silent movie careers, were pointedly silent. But when the talkies came he found he could project a rasping, imperious voice into the comedy which added a new dimension to it, and got more laughs. It also enabled him to articulate his hates, an increasingly important part of the W. C. Fields persona. Then, early in the thirties, he discovered radio. This followed a physical collapse, which forced him to dry out at Soboba Hot Springs. He had DTs and double vision in the hospital and found he could not read: his first intimations of mortality. Radio came as a godsend: "I lunged at it boldly and seized it by the throat with one hand, while tweaking its nose with the other."

He starred on the radio show Edgar Bergen made with his puppet, Charlie McCarthy, sponsored by Chase & Sanborn Coffee. Why this worked on radio is odd, but Fields found the puppet, neither a child nor a dog, uniquely hatable, and it made the show. Fields wrote the dialogue or ad-libbed. "I have a warm place for you, Charlie." "In your heart?" "No. In my fireplace." Charlie was "you animated hitching-post." Charlie called Fields "bugle-beak. Why don't you fill your nose with helium and rent it out as a barrage balloon?" He did his sketch "The Golf Game" with Charlie. Typical lines were "Will somebody get me a sedative with an olive in it?" "What's the score? How do I stand?" "Charlie, I often wonder." And: "Quiet, my termites' flop-house. I'll cut you down to a pair of shoe-trees."

Fields's battles with Charlie were fairly clean. But as a rule he had trouble with the censors. He never took the view that dirty jokes and innuendoes were beneath the dignity of a comic. An early impression in showbiz had been hearing Eva Tanguay sing "I Want Someone to Go Wild with Me" and "It's All Been Done Before But Not the Way I Do It," and discovering she got paid $3,000 a week. So Fields always used sex when he could get away with it. His battles with Joseph Breen, chief agent of the Hays Office, were an important part of showbiz history. The great point about Breen was that he had no sense of humor whatsoever, so Fields enjoyed the warfare. Much of

Breen's censorship survives, notably in *My Little Chickadee*.
"The goat must be cut." "We cannot have 'Willie of the Valley.'"
"Omit 'tramp' when applied to women." "Please cut the business of the woman belching." "Revealing white blouse must
go." "She must not expose her breasts." "Entire speech regard-
ing traveling salesman must go." "No suggestive movements in
scene with Indian." "No exposure in the bathtub." Breen hated
one of Mae West's favorite jokes: "She was Snow White, but
she drifted." Fields also lost "go back to the reservation and
milk your elk" and "pear-shaped ideas." Breen insisted: "Nix
the reference to Black Pussy Café. It would be acceptable to say
Black Pussy Cat Café." Breen objected to "physiology," "buz-
zards," "tighter than Dick's hat-band," and "Falling Water
O'Toole" as an Indian's name. Also censored were "showing
bananas and pineapples," "did you ever gondola?" and "playing
at Utsna." Breen would not have Fields "looking at girls' legs
and breasts and reacting thereto" or taking out false teeth. But
Fields, while accepting Breen's cuts, did not in fact carry them
out invariably. The goat stayed in, for instance.

Fields earned a lot of money and delighted to be thought
mean about it. What did he spend it on? One item was cars. At
one time he had seven, including big ones with traveling bars
in the back seats. He regarded a refrigerator in a car as "one
sign that civilization is worth having." He said, "Only fairies
ride in trains." At the funeral in 1942 of John Barrymore, who
died with only sixty cents in his pocket, Fields drove up in
his Cadillac with a bar fridge in the back. He brushed off
the boys admiring the vehicle at the graveyard gates: "Back to

the Reform School you little nose-pickers!" Once, when drinking in his car bar, a traffic cop pulled up: "You are double-parked." Fields: "No. We are sitting at the crossroads between Art and Nature, trying to figure out where Delirium Tremens leaves off and Hollywood begins." "That's OK, Mr. Fields."

Fields would never buy a house. He always rented. He had a saying: "All landlords should be sent to the electric chair." He refused to do repairs to his rented houses, preferring discomfort to doing his landlord a favor. His last (rented) house was 2015 De Mille Drive, near Griffith Park, Hollywood. It was gated, and had five bedrooms and eleven baths, and a maid's apartment (used by Carlotta, his mistress). It also had a "formal dining room," library, recording studio, glass elevator, a "full floor bar," tennis court, and observation deck. The rent was initially $250 a month, and when the landlord tried to raise it, Fields refused, even when the house began to fall apart. It had an exercise room, containing a stationary bike, a rowing machine, and "a bar well-stocked with potables." Carlotta later recorded, "At the sight of the bottles as an incentive, Woody would pedal furiously." His study was "cavernous" and contained "The W. C. Fields Filing System Desk." There he would "sit and type long, tipsy letters to friends." He had a big fridge on wheels with an endless electric cord so he could have ice for his drink in any room of the house. There was a barber's chair to relieve his back pain. The staff varied as Fields had rows with them. He had locks on all chests and strong room doors, "to stop the servants stealing my booze." But there was a permanent butler, a strong man known as "the Chimp."

In the last years of his life, 1940–1946, Fields enjoyed his quarrels more than ever, especially with servants: "In this house it's capital versus labor all the time." Animals aroused his fury. He chased away swans from his garden: "Either shit green, or get off the lawn." He believed his near neighbor, Deanna Durbin, the singing star of the famous musical movie *One Hundred Men and a Girl*, had trained the swans from her lake to invade his property. Another neighbor/enemy was Cecil B. De Mille. It was wartime and Fields had drunken fantasies about a Nazi invasion of California. His feud with De Mille came to a head one night with Fields growling "Why are you sneaking across my lawn with a warden's helmet on and carrying a shotgun? I believe you are a lost German paratrooper. You speak English well for a Nazi." "I was born here!" "I know. Another Benedict Arnold." "I pay your salary." "I know. Leave a check in the mailbox and beat a hasty retreat."

Fields claimed that in all the years he drank whiskey he never got drunk. Toward the end he switched to rum and pineapple juice. This was fattening. He hired a night watchman to drink with him until the small hours. He got DTs again: "I'd see the men with whiskers sitting on bulls. They'd charge me." Fields alternated between living at home and drying out in a bungalow at the Las Encinas clinic. His last recorded joke was an answer to the query "Do you like children?": "I do if they're properly cooked." His last appearance in a movie was 1945 and his final words as a performer were "Come, my little popinjay." But a $25 war bond was presented "to any nose which matches in size, color, and decorative effect the bulbous projection of Mr. Fields." In 1946 disease of the liver set in, and he moved permanently into his Encinas bungalow where he died over Christmas.

Humorists are either chaos-creators or order-enforcers. Fields had steered an unsteady course between the two. Instinctively he liked order. He was a U.S. marshal and a Los Angeles County deputy sheriff. But at his funeral on 2 January 1947 chaos finally took over. There were a lot of Hollywood people there and the famous boxer Jack Dempsey. Edgar Bergan gave the address. But also in attendance were Carlotta Monti and an angry ex-wife, Hattie Fields, as she called herself. There were in fact three memorial services: Catholic, attended by Hattie; spiritualist, conducted by the medium Mae Taylor; and a third when the casket was bricked up to await cremation. A tramp turned up who said he was an old pro who had known Fields for thirty-five years. Fields left $771,428, not counting sums stashed away in countless bank accounts. Among the claimants was a blind woman who said Fields had married her under a false name in 1893 when he was only thirteen, and an illegitimate son, William Rexford Field Wallace, who claimed his mother was a Ziegfeld chorus girl named Bessie Poole. He eventually got $15,000. Hattie Fields got most of the residue, but only after a seven-year legal battle, ending in 1954, by which time she was seventy-five.

Fields's story is not edifying. But it is not discouraging either, like that of so many comics. Since he took pleasure in fury, he got a lot out of life, and he gave a lot back too, in laughs. He always tried to be hard-boiled and cynical, brutal even. But there may have been another side. J. B. Priestley, the Yorkshire novelist, who had seen Fields as a silent juggler in the English halls before the First World War, and who recognized another Yorkshireman beneath his American skin, wrote of his tricks, "he moved warily in spite of a hastily assured air of nonchalant confidence, through a world in which even inanimate objects were hostile, rebellious, menacing, never to be trusted. He had to be able to *juggle* with things, to be infinitely more dextrous than you or I need be, to find it possible to handle them at all. They were not his things, these commonplace objects of ours. He did not belong to this world, but had arrived from some other and easier planet." But he was a hard man, all the same, perhaps precisely because he was unsure. His favorite line was "Never give a sucker an even break," and he meant it up to a point: the breaking point.

CHAPTER TEN

# CHARLIE CHAPLIN: SUPPLE, SUBTLE, AND SENTIMENTAL

CHARLIE CHAPLIN (1889–1977) remains enigmatic, though millions of words have been written about him. He is, perhaps, the most difficult of all the great comedians to sum up. At one time, around 1918, he was by far the most celebrated person alive, more famous than Woodrow Wilson or David Lloyd George or Ferdinand Foch or Lenin. Many experts in his field believed him to be the most accomplished comic of all time. These included Stan Laurel, himself a top-rank professional, who worked with Chaplin in the Fred Karno troupe and for a time shared lodgings with him. Chaplin remained famous for over sixty years and received all the honors possible. But he also inspired deep and irrational dislike, not only from public bodies, like the American government, but from those close to him.

Chaplin was scarred for life by a sad and impoverished childhood, which left him with monumental self-pity. "My father died when I was seven." "I have never had a day's schooling in my life." "My mother sewed blouses to keep us." "I never had a home worth the name." "When my mother died I was apprenticed to a company of traveling acrobats." None of these, and many other autobiographical statements of his, were true. He was born in East Street, Walworth, in south London. His father, also Charles, was a variety comedian, relatively successful but a drunkard: his parents separated when Charlie was a year old. But his father did not die when he was seven. His mother, Hannah, daughter of an Irish cobbler, a vaudeville singer under the name of Lily Harley, did not sew blouses but supported Charlie and his half brother, Sydney (son of an earlier South African lover) by her work on stage. He did have a home, and he did go to school. His mother, however, suffered from schizophrenia, was forced into the workhouse, and ended up in an insane asylum, living there for many years.

Chaplin's childhood, then, though distorted by his inventions, was pitiful enough: "Overshadowed by the pub, the doss-house and the bin." He was five foot four, and seemed even smaller, with tiny hands and feet. At eight he danced in the street for coppers. He was spotted by William Jackson, who ran a clog-dancing team called Eight Lancashire Lads. He arranged with Charlie's mother to take him on, give him board and lodging, and pay her half a crown (2s. 6d.) a week.

He thus was a cloggie for over two years, at a time when the music hall was at its zenith. He also worked in a barber's shop, a printing plant and a glass factory, and in other jobs, from all of which he got brilliant comic ideas. He was a natural actor, comedian, dancer, mimic, and musician (he learned to play a left-handed violin and wrote his own musical scores) of prodigious talent, and got material from any human activity.

However, Chaplin also received professional training from Fred Karno, probably the greatest instructor of every kind of comic talent who ever lived. He and his Speechless Comedians operated from a Fun Factory, which had its own small stage, rehearsal room, and property room, rather like the Tudor Revels Office in the sixteenth century. It also traveled, especially in America, and its heyday was 1904–1914. Karno, son of an itinerant cabinetmaker, had worked in every department of the theater and was especially skillful at training jugglers, acrobats, and farce clowns. His aim was to build up an act into a climax of total chaos, known as a Karno Picnic, the clue for which was his cry "Bring On the Dancing Girls." This, then, was Chaos Comedy, and Karno rehearsed it for weeks, even months, until every tiny action was perfect. He made a fetish of muscular control, from which Chaplin, above all his pupils, benefited most. Stan Laurel testified: "This was one of the most fantastically funny acts ever known—probably the greatest ensemble of the century." Karno required at least six months to train a comedian properly, and made Chaplin, said Laurel, "the most supple and precise comedian of our age," superb in his timing and movements. Chaplin was unpopular because he did not drink, saved his money, never carried cash (so he cadged from the other players), and did not speak "for weeks." But he had a set of smart clothes too. He was probably the most receptive of the Karno students and later used gags he learned in movie shorts (e.g., stamp licking, a surefire winner). Karno was mean but did not stint on important gags. Thus for his seasickness routine, he had made a stage ocean liner powered to rock by two hydraulic machines. Under Karno, Chaplin learned the use of really big stooges, such as Fred Kitchen, who emphasized his small size. He also learned funny walks in oversized shoes, and the simple but impressive trick of throwing a cigarette over his shoulder and kicking it offstage without looking. He later said: "The best gags are the simple ones which look easy but require the most rehearsal." He once showed Edmund Wilson his gag of shoving his bowler hat heavily down over his head, then having it pop into the air. "That's a difficult one. Try it for yourself."

Chaplin made two trips to America with Karno and did some summer theater, starring in Sherlock Holmes plays. His brother, Sydney, acted as his agent and was mercilessly bullied by him. But Chaplin, while recognizing Karno's brilliance as an ensemble-master and teacher, wanted independence. He was a creator, not an interpreter, and he thought Hollywood, then in formation, would offer him opportunities on film he could not get in the live theater. In 1913 he got an offer of $150 a week, then big money, from Keystone, under Mack Sennett, doing comic one-reelers. He was not happy, or funny, until he was allowed to pick his own gear—big shoes, tight jacket, baggy pants, tiny hat, moustache, and bent cane—and then think himself into the part. The part—a lonely, put-upon tramp, who embodied childhood miseries and current woes—came naturally. The virtue of the tramp role was that he could use it to display virtually any gag he had learned, and any new ones he could invent. He eventually acquired over fifty standard gags, with endless variations. The studio experts, who thought they knew all about motion pictures, could not understand his methods and requirements for endless rehearsal time and retakes. It was not until May 1914 that he was given the chance to make a one-reeler entirely on his own, with Keystone facilities. But during the next three years, with companies like First National, Mutual, and All Motion, he proved his carefully rehearsed and shot antics were excellent for the box office. He did not, like Byron, awake to find himself famous. He *made* himself famous, by unrelenting hard work, dedication, total selfishness, and genius. By the end of the First World War he had done it: millions of moviegoers were laughing at him all over the world. In New York, the Ziegfeld Follies had a song "Those Charlie Chaplin Feet." In Cleveland, Bob Hope, aged twelve, won a competition for the best Chaplin imitation, and bought his mother a new stove with the prize money. In London, Lupino Lane performed "That Charlie Chaplin Walk" in the musical *Watch Your Step*. There was the "Charlie Chaplin—March Grotesque," the "Charlie Chaplin Glide," the "Chaplin Waddle," all hit songs. Chaplin masks, hats, and canes sold in the gimmick shops. When he toured America and the world in those first years of fame, he was mobbed.

At the New York premiere of the Douglas Fairbanks hit movie *The Three Musketeers*, a woman used a pair of scissors to cut a piece off his trousers. He lost his tie, his collar, his waistcoat buttons, and the police had to carry him into the movie house. There were comparable scenes in the Place Pigalle in Paris, the French recognizing that "Charlot" was the first intellectual star to emerge from Hollywood, "one of us." Chaplin made a great deal of money, invested it shrewdly, and remained a rich man for the rest of his long life. He helped to form a self-governing studio, United Artists, with Mary Pickford, Fairbanks, and the director D. W. Griffiths, but even this eventually proved too restrictive. Thereafter Chaplin financed his own movies, as a rule, and (if he chose) produced and directed them, wrote the script and the music, and did personal distribution deals.

All the same, some of the best movies Chaplin ever made were done under studio control of a kind. *The Pawnshop* has a degree of curious detail which makes it worthy of close study. In *The Idle Class* he successfully abandoned the tramp role to play a millionaire. *Pay Day*, on a building site, makes classic use of a wooden elevator as a gag, and trick photography to show Chaplin doing an impossible turn catching bricks. There were two brilliant escaped convict films, *The Adventurer* and *The Pilgrim*. The last features a series of preacher gags on which Chaplin worked hard, and a brilliant sequence in which he turns his bowler hat into a pudding, which is eaten. (Stan Laurel remembered this when he ate his bowler hat in *Way Out West*.)

If one were asked to choose between Chaplin's silent shorts

and his later feature movies, the decision would be hard. It might depend on the group in which *The Kid* is placed. Chaplin was a loner who treated his coactors in an offhand manner. But *The Kid*, which many consider his greatest movie, would have been impossible without the child genius Jackie Coogan. He was only five years old and Chaplin found it a unique pleasure to work with him. Indeed he behaved like a mother with a child. He also fantasized: the movie has a strong autobiographical element, like Dickens's *David Copperfield*, so Jackie is Charlie himself, aged five, as filtered through the highly sentimental memory which Chaplin had constructed. No wonder Sigmund Freud was so interested in this movie, and considered Chaplin as a classic case of a major artist completely shaped by his childhood. The sentiment might be cloying, as so much of Chaplin's work is, but it is also, in this work, sincere and at times almost overpowering. The public certainly fell for it. The movie opened in 1921 and for the next three years enjoyed record receipts all over the world. Part of its success was due to Chaplin's skill in teaching Jackie how to mime, and also in editing. He cut four hundred thousand feet of film down to fifty-three hundred feet, and the movie is close to perfection in telling its story. In old age Chaplin saw it as the summit of his career and his best movie (but then at other times he said this of *City Lights*).

*The Gold Rush* is a compendium of clever gags which combine to create a satire on greed, avarice, and lust in a world where chaos rules. Hogarth would have loved it. Indeed it has some of his tricks, including a scene where a bear follows and chases Chaplin as a tramp figure. Much of the movie takes place in a log cabin which is almost organic, or living. Three basic psychological states are ruthlessly exploited: vertigo, when the entire cabin, sloping, teeters on the edge of a cliff; hallucination, when the hungry giant, Mark Swain, believes that Chaplin has become an edible chicken, helped by his brilliant fowl movements; and phantasmagoria, when Swain's boots are cooked, served, and eaten, with Chaplin acting as a superb stage-waiter. There is also a tumultuous dance scene of superlative comedy. The movie benefited enormously from Chaplin's freedom and independence. The sequence when, during a fight, the muzzle of a shotgun follows Chaplin mysteriously wherever he hides, required endless rehearsals and retakes. Again, Chaplin did the editing himself, reducing 231,503 feet of film to 8,490 feet. All this trouble and expense was justified by the takings: over $6 million gross, a record at the time, and by the way in which the picture still gets belly laughs nearly a century later. Chaplin said, "The best jokes are the simplest, and oldest. The finest stage direction ever is Shakespeare's, from *The Winter's Tale*: 'Exit, pursued by a bear.' That would get a laugh even if performed by Martians on the Moon to a tribe of Saturnines."

He liked *City Lights* too and sometimes called it his best movie. It takes up Stevenson's Jekyll and Hyde theme to show a millionaire who befriends the tramp when drunk and rejects him when sober, and in the process deals with illness, blindness, and madness. It confirms Evelyn Waugh's observation to Lady Diana Cooper, who feared she was losing her sight, that

"Blindness and madness in women has always had prodigious erotic appeal." Chaplin hated the heroine of the picture, Virginia Cherrill, a feeling which was eventually reciprocated. But he made her look enchanting as a blind woman. The movie is notorious for its opening sneer at patriotism—"the greatest insanity that the world has ever suffered"—and a pseudo-nude in a shop window. Indeed it is replete with weird tricks, including a mesmeric jaywalking sequence. The picture made Einstein cry, and he allowed himself to be photographed with Chaplin in a publicity shot, but protected by the formidable Frau Einstein.

*Modern Times* is the best known of Chaplin's movies, partly because of the brilliant stills showing him being processed through the giant cogwheels. The idea of modernity transforming human beings into machines was not new. It goes back to early Victorian times, and was given a classic formulation in Henri Bergson's *Le rire*: "The attitudes, gestures and movements of the human body are laughable in exact proportion so that body reminds us of a mere machine." But nobody ever went to such trouble and expense to show this principle in action. The movie is an attack on industrial capitalism and embodied the notion of everyone being watched by the State Leviathan that George Orwell was later to call Big Brother. Chaplin ignored the fact that the principle was already in action in Stalin's Russia. His unwillingness ever to criticize Communism was his greatest moral failure and a tremendous missed opportunity. As it was, he worked in some wonderful gags. So that workers could continue to operate machines during mealtimes, the corporation created a feeding machine. The sequence in which the machine forced Chaplin to eat the corncob at top speed and wipes his mouth with a napkin, ending with it forcing him to eat metal balls and giving him a shave, is brilliantly conceived and faultlessly realized. So is the sequence in which he tightens screws for security and ends up in the machine itself. The original title was *The Masses*. This was changed to *Modern Times*, a much better name, to please organized Catholic opinion. But the movie was banned in Nazi Germany and Fascist Italy. All the American censors objected to were a close-up of a cow's udders, a bra gag, an anti-queer joke, and references to "stomach-rumblings" and "dope." But though a huge success worldwide, the movie's earnings in the United States were less than *City Lights*, *The Gold Rush*, and even the comparative failure, *The Circus*.

The truth is, Chaplin never willingly came to terms with the talkies, though his skillful use of music, often written or edited by himself as a perfect match for the action, concealed his failure. He was essentially a mime; a mimic. Unable to resist sound in the end, he was forced to abandon the Tramp, who makes a final appearance in the last shot of *Modern Times*, walking with his back to the camera into infinity. He speaks a few words right at the end but his only personal use of sound in the movie is when he sings a nonsense song as a waiter in the café scene:

Ce rakish spacoletto
Si la tu, la tu, la tua!

Senora pelafima
Vouley-vous le taximeter?

But even here the magic of the words is overshadowed by Chaplin's superb movements, including the backward foot slide, the twinking buttocks shot, and the curvy hand massage, all of which he had long since honed to perfection.

Critics have argued that *Modern Times*, which ought to have been Chaplin's masterpiece, on account of the new ideas it contains, suffered from his freedom. He had no one to supervise him or correct his obsessions and self-indulgencies. In art, freedom tends to corrupt, and absolute freedom corrupts, if not absolutely, then seriously. The combination of talkies and freedom meant that Chaplin's later movies were never quite so good as his masterworks of the twenties and early thirties.

If Chaplin had been younger and less successful, and so less set and complacent in his ways, he might have realized he was a master of sound as well as movement and taken full advantage of the funny opportunities the sound track offered him. His use of "jabber" was perfect, and in private life Chaplin often kept visitors and dinner-party guests convulsed with impromptu utterances. Not knowing a word of Chinese, he could do a marvelous imitation of a Chinaman, or even two, conversing at top speed. He could do Eskimo grunt-speech (accompanied by gobbling of candles and soap) and Congolese mumbo jumbo. He did a wonderful South Seas cannibal feast scene, working in haute cuisine references and *Michelin Guide* terms. He also specialized in fake lectures: "Some Doubts as to the Origins of Species" (with a marvelous gag about evolution going backward), "The Benefits of Birth Control" by a lady based upon Mrs. Emmeline Pankhurst, and "Some Benefits of the New Deal" in Eleanor Roosevelt's voice. Some of his efforts in private were maniacal, and give substance to his evident fear that he could go insane like his mother. His skill suggests he did suffer (mildly) from schizophrenia. Stan Laurel put his finger on it: "Charlie was a wonderful mixture: a shy and timid man who continually mustered up the courage to do adventurous and wonderful things." He could burlesque the final scene in *Camille* and die of TB. He did a wicked imitation of Truman Capote breakfasting at Tiffany's and proposing to an eighteen-year-old virgin over the eggs Benedict. Although Chaplin was athletic and loved tennis, he was hopeless at golf but could do a masterly sketch of General Eisenhower playing it while discoursing on the Middle East in his mangled English. Other party tricks were "Schopenhauer talking philosophy in High German," "Gary Cooper Thinking" (silent), and "Clark Gable taking out his false teeth" (very horsey). But Chaplin's most beautiful imitations were of flowers or trees.

All his life, Chaplin was plagued by intense sexual desires which repeatedly got him into trouble. He loved very young girls, or girls who looked like boys with cropped hair and wearing short pants. This propensity to prefer underage girls to the big-bosomed floozies who were in plentiful supply was a feature of early Hollywood, and may be one reason why the state of California at this time treated statutory rape (inter-course with a girl under sixteen with or without her consent) so severely: in some cases it carried a twenty-year mandatory sentence. He and D. W. Griffith competed for girls/children of fourteen, or those who just looked it. In *The Birth of a Nation*, Griffith gave the two best female parts to Lillian Gish, who was seventeen, and to Mae Marsh, just eighteen. Chaplin liked to "score," as he put it, with these teenagers; a dangerous game, for most had watchful mothers in the background, quite capable of blackmail. The girls themselves were skilled at entrapment in all its varieties. Chaplin's first marriage, in 1918, to Mildred Harris, was certainly involuntary on his part. Described as "very small, like a little doll," she could look thirteen, and was quite prepared to swear it for legal purposes. Her actual age was eighteen at the time she married Chaplin. His second marriage, to another baby doll, might be described in Dr. Johnson's words, as the triumph of hope over experience. Lita Grey's actual name, curiously enough, was Lilita. She first crossed Chaplin's path during the filming of *The Kid*, when she was twelve. She featured in a dream sequence, exposing her ankle to tempt him around a corner where he is shot by her "fiancé."

Chaplin was tempted by her in real life, finally seducing her in a bathroom three years later. A lavish bathroom, thanks to the luxury decor of Cecil B. De Mille, was a room dedicated to Venus. Such a setting excited Chaplin, who had succeeded in seducing Gloria Swanson in one. Lita promptly became pregnant, and her mother, just as promptly, moved from background to foreground, accompanied by Lita's uncle, lawyer, and accountant, described by Chaplin as "a bloody bunch of money-hungry scum." Lita was still only sixteen when they married. His third wife, the delectable Paulette Goddard, also looked "like a little girl," and played a gamin role in *Modern Times*. But she was actually twenty-two. Her real name was Pauline Marion Goddard Levy, and they were married in a synagogue; whether Chaplin was Jewish, as has often been asserted, has never been finally established. In any event, Paulette proved a kind stepmother to the two sons Chaplin had by Lita, and then in due course made a graceful exit from his life.

There were many other "scores." They included the ferocious Rebecca West, one-time mistress of H. G. Wells, and the fine period piece Louise Brooks, who many years later provided curious details about Chaplin's sexual concepts, including his practice of painting his penis and testicles with iodine in the belief it was a sure protecting agent against VD. She also gave an account of a foursome she shared with Chaplin, a Follies girl named Peggy Fears, and the financier A. C. Blumenthal. Brooks took Chaplin's decision to move on in good part: "He didn't give me a [farewell] fur from Jaeckel or a bangle from Cartier, just a nice check in the mail." She also testified that he was one of the most baffling and complex men who ever lived. Pola Negri, who had an affair with Chaplin in the 1920s, said, "His ability to bring out maternal feelings was one of his greatest assets with the opposite sex." He himself said, "There should never be any need to chase a girl round the bed. The affair begins when you say 'Good afternoon.'"

He married his fourth wife, Oona, daughter of the American-Irish playwright Eugene O'Neill, in 1943 and the marriage lasted until his death thirty-four years later. She gave him three sons and five daughters, and the marriage was accounted happy. It was at least durable. One reason was that their home was in Switzerland, whence Chaplin had retreated after he was denied reentry into the United States for political reasons (he had kept his British citizenship). So Chaplin was no longer plagued by child starlets on the make. Moreover, the Chaplins lived near the hideous villa owned by the copious writer of *policiers*, Georges Simenon, a far more persistent, and less discriminating womanizer than Chaplin. Indeed he claimed to have slept with twenty-eight hundred women. His wife, Denyse, poured out her problems to Oona, including Simenon's habit of picking the housemaids for their looks, so he could enjoy seducing them, provoking one to ask Denyse, "Ici, on passé toutes à la casserole?" What Oona objected to, in the aging Chaplin, was his long-winded habit of telling her about past scores. "All those old bags he slept with! I'm sick of hearing about them. . . . What am I supposed to do when he's talking like that? Sit there and smile and simper?" Instead she took to the bottle, which made her widowhood a sad affair.

But then, where is the comedian or humorist whose life is not sad, in part anyway? Chaplin was lucky in many ways: always rich, always courted and honored and listened to, with a huge oeuvre of movies to look back on. But it is a fact that after *Modern Times* (1936) he never made a first-class movie. I recall seeing *The Great Dictator* (1940) when it was first released in England. I was eleven at the time and much disappointed. My elders said Chaplin had missed many opportunities to make

Hitler funny, and I agreed with them. It seemed odd to me that he allowed the Mussolini character to score off Hitler, for it was already apparent that he was the real joke figure. Jack Oakie, who played Musso (or, rather, Napaloni), carried off the movie, if anyone did. Chaplin's later movies, *Monsieur Verdoux* (1947), *Limelight* (1952), *A King in New York* (1957), and *A Countess from Hong Kong* (1967), were rarely funny, though never without a certain professional and historical interest.

Chaplin's last joke was played inadvertently after his death. On 1 March 1978, nine weeks after he was buried, it was found his coffin had been dug up and stolen from the cemetery at Vevey, near his Swiss home. A sum of 600,000 Swiss francs was demanded for its return. The two guilty clowns, who might have played in a Mack Sennett farce seventy years before, were soon caught, tried, convicted, and sentenced. A cross was erected in the field where the stolen coffin was found. Oona visited it—a strange memorial to Chaplin's strange life.

# CHAPTER ELEVEN

# LAUREL AND HARDY: ERA OF GOOD FOOLING

O N 16 JUNE 1890 Arthur Stanley Jefferson was born at Ulverston, Lancashire, on the edge of the Lake District. Eighteen months later, Novell Hardy was born on 18 January 1892, in Harlem, Georgia. These two men both changed their names to become Stan Laurel and Oliver Hardy. They were unique in becoming a comedy duo in which each made an equal contribution to the humor. They were also unique in the consistently high quality of the clowning, reaching at times a sublimity amounting to genius. Both were chaos men, and in combination produced degrees of disorder and tumultuous frays which even Fred Karno, who trained Laurel, the brains of the outfit, never bettered. They created their chaos scenes by an unintentional competition in stupidity, the secret of their popularity: in their stupidity, so various, so bottomless, so dependable, lay their genius. They were also so reliably innocent. There was no nastiness, no malice, no crude or dirty jokes, no hidden agenda, no politics, no indoctrination, no violence; nobody got really hurt, though a variety of ingenious sound effects made Hardy, who as fat man was the traditional fall guy in clowning, appear to take hard knocks. Behind their professional partnership lay mutual respect and affection. Hardy, who regarded himself as a mere comic actor, was quite content to allow Laurel to write scripts, devise gags, and direct (on occasion) their movies, and was never jealous when, in consequence, Laurel earned much more than he did. Laurel acknowledged Hardy's extraordinary skills at getting laughs, and in old age, after Hardy died in 1957 and before his own death in 1965, would sit watching his old movies, especially the silent ones of 1927 to 1933, laughing uproariously at Hardy's antics.

Laurel was in show business from the age of ten. His father was a theater manager in a small way, his mother an actress. Aged nineteen he joined the Karno troupe and went to America. Hardy's connection with movies began aged eighteen in 1910 when he ran the Electric Theater in Milledgeville, Georgia. Both men were in movies some years, acting separately, in New York and Florida—Hardy played heavies, Laurel a variety of parts—before coming together at the Hal Roach Studio, apparently, in 1926. Thereafter they worked mainly for Roach but also for Arrow Pictures, L-KO Studios, King Bee, Lubin, Vitagraph, and Vim Comedies, as well as MGM. Their first duo, *Duck Soup*, was released in March 1927. It has nothing to do with the Marx Brothers movie of the same name, other than the fact that neither features duck or any other soup in the action. The Laurel and Hardy movie was based on a sketch written by Laurel's father in 1905, called "Home from the Honeymoon." This film illustrates that obscure continuities in showbiz are infinite: the only copy of this movie disappeared for half a century until it was discovered in a Belgian archive.

The two began working together regularly in 1927 and made a hit as soon as they both adopted bowler hats (initially Hardy wore a top hat and monocle). The bowler hat was of huge symbolic and practical importance in their movies (like the gray topper for W. C. Fields) and went with their tailcoats and boiled shirts. They were not tramps but members of the middle class hovering on the verge of respectability, and their strong desire for security and regular employment, as opposed to the chaos their idiocy created, was a key part of their appeal. They never deliberately caused trouble: on the contrary, it is precisely their desire to do well which brings disaster. One of Karno's rules for comic acting was the need to establish roles and stick to them: "The audience likes to know where they are, and to be sure of the characters." Laurel was content to allow professional scriptwriters to devise scenarios and comic situations. But he insisted on preserving the integrity of each character in the duo. Most of the gags were his, or rather part of his comic heritage going back hundreds of years.

Effectively, Laurel and Hardy were reliable at the box office for a quarter of a century. They crossed the boundary from movies to talkies with aplomb, for both developed excellent speaking voices, perfectly in character. Their work speaks for itself. But three items call for particular attention. One of the early silent shorts, *The Battle of the Century*, survives only in a damaged print with bits missing. The original "battle" was a boxing match with Laurel as the hopeless champ, Canvasback, and Hardy as his coach. After he loses, the two drift into a situation where they become involved in a pie fight. This becomes the real battle of the century, taking one of the oldest of slapstick gags and developing it on a heroic scale, with literally dozens of pies flying through the air and finding unwitting faces to hit. There are a dozen scintillating vignettes of pies hitting their targets, such as men in barber's and dentist's chairs, and elegant women getting out of limos. The great fat actor Eugene Palette is one participant. So is the plump boy later to star in Abbott and Costello movies. There is a superb cinematic moment when a beautiful society lady gets a custard pie up her skirt but carries on gracefully as if nothing had happened. Her name remains unknown, as do those of the other witty participants in this hilarious sequence, a fitting climax to the last phase of the silent cinema, one of the great comic art forms of history.

*We Faw Down*, another silent short, features gold digger types, a pestilential tribe of women from whom both Laurel and Hardy suffered in real life. In both this and in *Block-Heads*, the old gag, first used by Hogarth, of an adulterer escaping, without his breeches, through a window, is used with as much thoroughness and brio as the custard pie. When Hardy inadvertently lets off a shotgun, bedroom windows in an entire street open up and men without their pants jump down from each and run for it. This sequence took a great deal of rehearsal and many retakes to get the jumping exactly synchronized, for twenty trouserless men were involved. Exact timing was at all times paramount in these movies.

*Dirty Work* is an early talkie in which Laurel and Hardy play two sweeps. They "do" the home of Professor Noodle, who is doing research into rejuvenation, and has a huge tank filled with the precious fluid, whose final perfection he reaches just as the sweeps begin work. They press up the chimney and wreck it, and on the roof there is a brilliant panoramic shot of early 1930s Los Angeles, since this short, like many others, was made on cheap location, not in the studio. Laurel's clumsiness leads Hardy to exclaim, "You do your work. I'll do mine. I have nothing more to say." The last sentence becomes a running gag. The butler, Jessop, surveying the wreckage, says darkly, "Somewhere, an electric chair is waiting." In the final sequence, Laurel by accident pushes Hardy into the rejuvenation tank, and the huge quantity of the magic fluid, as opposed to the tiny injection Noodle intended, turns Hardy into a victim of Darwin's theory of evolution in reverse, and he emerges as a chimpanzee. But he retains his bowler hat, and when a terrified Laurel says, "Speak to me, Ollie," replies, "I still have nothing to say." The brilliant tricks with which this last bit, with a live chimp, and Hardy's voice, were made are not recorded.

Thanks to Laurel's perfectionism, the result of his Karno training, supporting parts in their movies, for silent and talkie, were nearly always well filled. In *Dirty Work*, Lucien Littlefield makes an excellent mad professor, and Sam Adams, a sad, resigned butler. The duo particularly needed actors to play explosive dignitaries exasperated by their destructive antics. In *The Music Box*, the only item in the duo's work to be acknowledged by the Hollywood establishment, winning the 1932 Oscar for best short subject comedy, the duo, playing horse-and-cart deliverymen, take a piano, in its wooden box, up the 131 steps of Vendome Street, instead of going around the proper way by road. This actually exists, in the Silver Lake district of Los Angeles, and the whole movie was shot on location. When they finally deliver the piano, they comprehensively wreck the house it is to adorn. The angry owner, a professor, played by Billy Gilbert, gives them a fine rage scene. Gilbert also does a rage outburst in *County Hospital*, where Laurel gets the head surgeon suspended hundreds of feet over the street, in the wire apparatus used to hold up Hardy's plastered leg. But the most frequent, and successful, supporting player for the duo was the brilliant Scotch performer James Finlayson. He first appeared on the scene in 1923, and made a score of movies with them. He played hotel managers, prison governors, saloon bar owners, and other authority figures annoyed by their antics. He could screw up his eyes in the most striking manner to express rage, as well as cunning, greed, revenge, and general animosity. As the saloon owner, he helped to turn *Way Out West* into by far the best feature-length talkie the duo made; indeed, one of the best motion pictures of all time.

This film is notable for two songs which bring out the duo's extraordinary skills. When they arrive in Brushwood Gulch, they discover a hillbilly band singing that catchy number "After the Ball—That's All." They break into an impromptu dance on the steps of the saloon. Hardy, like some fat men (he weighed over three hundred pounds), had small feet on which he moved with serene dignity. Laurel had danced since he was tiny. The pair, in their dusty tailcoats and bowler hats, perform a dance of such exquisite grace as to constitute one of the great moments of the cinema. Later, inside the saloon, at the bar, they sing a soulful, Western ditty, "On the Trail of the Lonesome Pine." Hardy had a fine high tenor voice, which he uses to great effect in this number, and to match it, Laurel sings a verse first in falsetto then, after Hardy hits him on the head with a mallet, in contrabass. They made this fine song famous, and it usually gets into the hit charts whenever *Way Out West* is shown on TV at Christmas. The movie is also notable for a tickling scene, in which Laurel revels hysterically. The duo, who avoided scatological humor as beneath them, never gave the censors any trouble, and this may be the reason why this weirdly erotic sequence was passed without a murmur.

Not that Laurel and Hardy, either separately or together, were antiwomen. Quite the reverse. They were constantly, and foolishly, involved with them in private life, much to the delight of the Hollywood gossip columnists and headline writers, who followed their periodic marriages and divorces with relish. They were constantly involved, sometimes legally, sometimes not, with women named Lois, Mae, Myrtle, and Lucille, some of them interchangeable visually, at least to modern eyes. Women named Virginia, far from virginal, frequently popped up in their marital prosopology. So far as I can find out, events went as follows. Laurel's first wife was Mae Dahlberg. Hardy's first wife was Madelyn Salushin. He divorced her, married Myrtle Reeves. Laurel divorced Mae, remarried her, then divorced her again to marry Lois Neilson Ozmun. Hardy divorced Madelyn. Laurel divorced Lois, then married Virginia Ruth Rogers, not once but twice. Hardy married another woman named Myrtle, then divorced her. Laurel had two years of divorce court battles with Virginia Ruth. Then he married Vera Ivanova Shuvalova, known as Illiana, not once but three times. Then they were divorced. Hardy married Lucille Virginia Jones. Then Laurel remarried Virginia Ruth, divorced her again five years later, then married Ida Kitaeva. These events took place between 1923 and 1946. Hardy died in 1957, still married (I think) to Virginia. Laurel died in 1965, still married (I think) to Ida. Some of these women can be seen in their silent movies, and one or two had speaking or onlooker parts in their talkies. As Laurel and Hardy made several shorts featuring screen wives, sometimes played by real ones, and because each, and sometimes both, appeared in drag, the picture is confused. But as Hardy once said, in an inspired moment, "Life is not confused, if you know how. But it is muddled." "Then it's your fault," said Laurel. Their women, in their movies and in real life alike, were pretty but aggressive. A typical one was Dorothy Coburn, who plays the angry nurse in *The Finishing Touch* who is annoyed when the noise made by Laurel and Hardy, clumsy builders, disturbs the nearby hospital where she works. At one point she lands her formidable right fist in Hardy's solar plexus, a blow that certainly looks real. But she finishes in their whitewash pit, as does the friendly cop, played by Edgar Kennedy, after he submits to being covered in instant glue, to which slate tiles adhere tenaciously. This is a brilliant talkie, culminating in a frantic sequence of chaos, when an escaped steamroller entirely demolishes the house which the duo had been "finishing."

This was a real house, paid for by the studio, on a real building estate. It was often cheaper to work this way than to construct an imitation house on the set. In *Big Business*, the archetypical Laurel and Hardy destruction comedy, they are attempting to sell a Christmas tree, in the back of their car, to James Finlayson, who owns a house on a new estate. He does not want a tree. They persist in trying to sell it to him. In the dispute that follows, he progressively demolishes their car, while they demolish his house. It is a convention of these ruin scripts that neither party does anything except watch while the other carries out destructive acts. The studio had a car which could be "destroyed" and put together again. But for the house, they bought one. The shooting took an entire day, and at the end of it, a couple arrived, and claimed that the now demolished house was theirs. They had just bought it, and the one the studio owned, still intact, was next door. Alas, the cameras had stopped running, and there is no record of this touching scene. I believe a similar muddle occurred in *Tit for Tat*, but I do not know the details.

There are many missing bits in the story of Laurel and Hardy, as well as missing feet of film. The ravishing Rosina Lawrence, who plays the servant-made-heiress in *Way Out West*, and rides off in triumph with them at the end (and, incidentally, segued in the high voice when Laurel sings falsetto to "The Lonesome Pine"), was never seen again. What happened to her? No one knows. Some of Laurel's best gags are mysteries too. Simple comic acting, marvelously carried out and timed, explains the success of his production of a glass of water from his right pocket, and cubes of ice from his left, to make a highball. Similar means ensure the success of his eating his hat, when he produces pepper from his right waistcoat pocket, and salt from his left. It is the same when he pulls down the shadow of a blind on a wall—probably an old Karno gag. But how does he light an invisible pipe, producing the flame by flicking his thumb? He uses this gag several times, and it always works, enhanced by the amazed expression on Hardy's face.

These faces, direct to camera, were Hardy's forte. If first used by Hogarth, or even by Shakespeare, they became his personal property, and no comic actor has ever employed them with more variety and skill. They were something the cinema could convey much better than the stage. The cinema close-up also enables us to realize how skillful Hardy was with his hand and wrist movements, which beautifully conveyed a variety of emotions and moods, especially decision, derision, and finality. No film actor rewards careful scrutiny more.

Curiously enough, the best piece of joint comedy Laurel and Hardy ever performed was their destruction act with a girl named Lupe Vélez, known as "The Mexican Spitfire." This combined the mutual venting of rage with their attitude to aggressive women, the objects destroyed being not houses or cars but fresh eggs, found in a bowl on a bar, and normally used for eggnog. In turn, and with the duo and the girl each passively watching while being abused, in accordance with their strict formula, eggs are broken over their persons, and in their pockets and between Lupe's cleavage. The timing adds to the tension, and is perfect. The use of eggs is crucial because all three are doing what the audience secretly longs to do. This sequence, dating from 1934, is included in what was known as a "portmanteau film," to which stars from a particular studio contributed. It is hard to find and I treasure my copy. No one ever surpassed these two hardworking and estimable men in producing harmless fun to brighten the darker days of life. Why there was all the marrying and divorcing is a mystery, and perhaps belongs to a different life.

CHAPTER TWELVE

# THE MARX BROTHERS: SECOND LAW OF THERMODYNAMICS

O F ALL THE comics throughout history who have cre-
ated chaos to raise laughs, the Marx Brothers—Leonard
"Chico" Marx (1887–1961), Adolph or Arthur "Harpo" Marx
(1888–1964), Julius Henry "Groucho" Marx (1890–1977),
Herbert "Zeppo" Marx (1901–1979), and the brothers' manager, Milton "Gummo" Marx (1897–1977)—were the most
dedicated, refined, and successful. And the most hardheaded.
I once interviewed Groucho Marx for Associated-Rediffusion
Television, in the old Studio 9 at the bottom of London's
Kingsway. Afterward we talked. I asked, "What makes
comedy?" He answered, "Money." He said, "Farce is always
expensive, even on the stage. In movies it is very expensive
because you need so many rehearsals to get the timing exactly

right, and even then you need endless retakes. You have to shoot a hell of a lot of film to give the editors a chance. With big crews, at union rates, and perfectionist directors and editors, that means huge wage-bills. But then at the end you have a cinematic work of art which lasts for ever. It's an investment. But the guys who control the industry now [1963] are not interested in long-term investment. Quick profit is what they want. We could not make a movie like *A Night at the Opera* now. Too expensive."

Comedy is a form of physics. It is very "physical." Chaos comedy proceeds according to the second law of thermodynamics, the entropy principle. Entropy is a measure of the degree of disorder or randomness in the system. In chaos comedy human intervention accelerates entropy. You might say the Marx Brothers system is an antichaos theory: a study of complex systems whose behavior is highly sensitive to slight changes which provoke large consequences. Chaos cannot be created without order in the first place, since order, or zero entropy, begins the entire process of declension. For the Marx Brothers, order was represented by their mother, Minnie Marx, a professional showbiz booking manager, who taught her sons how to drive hard bargains, and how to force management to stick to them. They drove the hardest bargain with MGM in the history of the studio. The executive who conceded this was Irving Thalberg, but the strength of the Marx Order Principle was so powerful that L. B. Mayer, the ultimate boss, endorsed the bargain, which gave the brothers 15 percent "off the top," that is of gross profits. This gave the brothers a degree of financial security which enabled them to argue with MGM on equal terms about the financing of particular movies. Thus the budgets enabled them to create the chaos which eventually brought top box office returns and continues to do so. That in turn meant order in the accounts. Thus Marxian entropy went: order, disorder, order. Thalberg didn't always see it that way. Groucho told me, "He'd call us and say, 'What do you guys think you are doing? Do you think money grows on trees?' I'd say, 'Yessir. Money does grow on trees—MGM trees.'" If necessary they could subject Thalberg to chaos theory. Being orderly themselves when not on professional duty, they expected Thalberg to keep appointments to see them on time. If he kept them waiting, being himself chaotic when busy, they would blow cigar smoke under his door, pile filing cabinets against it, or, if he was late arriving, roast potatoes in his fireplace. No scientists were more adamant in following principles to the bitter entropic end.

The brothers employed some of the wittiest scriptwriters Hollywood could provide in its golden age, including George S. Kaufman, S. J. Perelman, and Bert Kalmar. But they wrote a lot of their own lines. Chico specialized in mispronunciation. Groucho (in *The Cocoanuts*): "We're going to have an auction." Chico: "I came over here on the Atlantic Auction." Or, from *A Night at the Opera*, during the contract-signing scene, Chico says, "You can't fool me. There ain't no sanity clause" (Santa Claus). Groucho used this device too: "If you can't leave in a taxi, you can leave in a huff. If that's too soon you can leave in a minute and a huff" (half). Other Groucho lines: "I never forget a face but I'll make an exception in your case." "I've been around so long I can remember Doris Day before she became a virgin." "Any man who says he can see through a woman is missing a lot." "A man is as young as the woman he feels." "My name isn't Groucho. I'm breaking it in for a friend." When excluded from a California beach club: "Since my daughter is half-Jewish, can she get in up to her knees?" Part of the business of creating chaos was the generation of a feeling of unease and approaching catastrophe. The Marx Brothers did this in various ways, each peculiar to its author. Harpo oscillated between his sexual maniac persona, making sudden grabs at the chorus girls, and his ecstatic master-musician harping, "putting on his Mozart-in-Heaven face." Chico did his peculiar piano playing which he devised and perfected himself. Both Harpo's harping and Chico's piano playing were peculiarly offensive and unsettling to "proper" players. Groucho's phony moustache and his sloping walk were also disturbing and produced an initial nervousness as a prelude to chaos making.

It was of the essence of Marx Brothers humor that, while generating unease, they claimed there was a conspiracy to unsettle them. Harpo claimed noise prevented him from practicing his harp each morning, then said, "This place is so quiet you can scarcely hear an anvil drop." He smoked cigars, then quit; he gambled, then quit; he only drank alcohol once, didn't like it, then quit; he quit speaking during performances, but operated inanimate objects to make his point. He could not remember names, and called everyone Benson: "Miss Benson, meet Mr. Benson." It is a sure form of humor to make big things seem trivial. The Marx Brothers' form was to make trivial things seem huge. Thus Groucho: "The next thing is, you'll be asking me to lend you a match."

An important part was played in their movies by the statu-esque actress Margaret Dumont. She played the society bene-factress whose wealth was an engine of the plot: tall, well mannered, dignified, and immobile, she stood for the princi-ple of order. Groucho scurried around her, accompanied by his two destructive brothers, creating chaos, which drew from the lady's shock, horror, distress, tolerance, and forgiveness. Then the cycle could begin again. She was needed, in order to be shocked. She was also needed to reassure the audience that all the destruction was playacting—property was not really being wrecked, and nobody was getting really hurt. Chaos comedy only works if those watching it feel safe in the knowledge that it's just a story. But the chaos has to be filmed to look as real as possible to give the story power. Chaos humor requires veri-similitude.

The person who understood this best, in the silent movie era, was Buster Keaton. He went to considerable lengths, when in charge of his own work, to achieve absolute real-ism in his gags, especially the life-imperiling ones. He often took frightening risks, as when he had the wall of a house col-lapse around him, missing him with a calculated clearance of only two inches. A lot of his destruction-shots were also real. Thus, in *The General*, his greatest movie, a real train crashes through a real bridge. This single shot cost $40,000, the most expensive shot in the entire silent era. *The General* lost money when originally released, but is now regarded as a classic and a major work of art. Keaton's insistence on expensive realism undermined his career, and led to his break with MGM. He was glad to get work with the up-and-coming Marx Brothers, devising gags for them and writing scripts. According to Groucho, he reinforced their conviction that imaginary chaos was funniest when it was most realistic.

The brothers made superb chaos scenes in *Duck Soup* and *A Day at the Races*. But their greatest piece of chaos art was the cabin scene in *A Night at the Opera*. This involved getting an enormous number of people, and things, into a small cabin onboard a transatlantic ship going to New York, all of them continuing to do their work as if nothing unusual was happening. This has claims to be considered the greatest item in the entire history of the cinema. Like most of the Marx Brothers' best gags, this was an exercise in philosophical physics: in this case, logistics. What precisely the term conveys is open to dispute. French military theory insists it consists of three parts: strategy, tactics, and logistics. The third stands for everything to do with armies which come under the quartermaster—supplies, food, barracks, transport, etc. Hence modern transport firms claim they are "experts in logistics," a word which features prominently in their advertising and promotion. But a narrower definition insists that the etymology of the word comes from the reign of Louis XIV in France. The *maître de logis* was the high official charged with the task of lodging

THE MARX BROTHERS 171

the troops, or the itinerant court. Hence it means getting the largest number of people, or goods, into the smallest possible space, without killing or damaging them. The cabin scene is thus a brilliant display of logistics and the chaos comes to a natural and indeed scientific end when the door busts open and everyone (and everything) spills into the corridor. This illustrates the point in entropy when there is no alternative in physics to the big bang which created the universe. Of course the cabin scene, as Groucho explained to me, was very expensive, in both rehearsal and shooting time, let alone editing. "L. B. Mayer shouted at me, 'What are you guys trying to prove?'" The true answer, of course, was one aspect of quantum theory. But Groucho did not know this at the time. Chaplin's *The Kid* made Einstein cry. But that was sentiment. The Marx Brothers made him think. That was physics.

In Groucho's moral universe (and all great comics have one), the destructive business of creating chaos was justified by its fascinating uncertainty—what the poet Keats called "negative capability." But Groucho also had a strong moral principle, illustrated by his assertion that "I don't want to belong to a club which would have me as a member." He was making an important philosophical point, which robustly adds another dimension to the Marx Brothers' chaos theory. It is arguable that the urge to perfection is exactly balanced by the consciousness of imperfection. Belonging to the perfect club is thus impossible to the altruistic. I think this is a logical conundrum invented by Bertrand Russell, and known as "the set of sets." I am aware that Russell liked the Marx Brothers because he told me so. But he cannot have been aware of Groucho's club problem while writing his *Principia mathematica* before the First World War. Does it matter? Groucho's dilemma is a real one. It indicates the fact that the exploration of comedy takes one up to, and into, some of the deepest mysteries of existence.

# CHAPTER THIRTEEN

# JAMES THURBER: RAISING A LAUGH BY ACCIDENT

T HERE ARE SOME aspects of humor which do not respond to logic, let alone physics. That is where James Thurber (1894–1961) comes in. His maternal grandfather was a huge blacksmith named Jacob Fisher, so strong he could pick up a horse. This is stated as a historical fact, though it is not explained how, or by what, he picked the horse up. Or how often he did so, or for what purpose. Or whether it was always the same horse, or different ones. His grandfather was an eccentric greengrocer, with many odd sisters, Thurber's great-aunts. His mother, Mary Agnes Fisher, was born in 1866 and grew up to be eccentric too. Her speciality was practical jokes. She wanted to be a comic actress, and liked to pretend to casual visitors that she was kept a prisoner in the attic because she wanted to marry the postman. Her actual husband, Thurber's father, a clerk who worked for and backed political losers, was a nobody who lived in Columbus, Ohio. In 1901, when Thurber was six, his brother William shot an arrow into his left eye. The injury was not treated properly. Not only did he lose his left eye, but "sympathetic opthalmia" developed in the right one, and in middle age he gradually became blind. He had himself made a pair of glass eyes, with which to amuse, astonish, and frighten people, when he fitted them in. One had the stars and stripes on it. He was nearly six foot two and could look formidable, especially when he was angry, which was often.

Thurber did not work out a precise theory of humor. Indeed precision, in any field, was a quality he did not possess. He might be described as "purposefully vague." He saw the world through a mist in which objects loomed, and on closer investigation turned out to be not the familiar ones you expected, but quite different things. Quantum theory, in which exactitude is impossible to attain, appealed to him. In this respect he was a characteristic figure of the twenties. When the *New Yorker* was founded in 1925 by Harold Ross, Thurber logically (or, to be more accurate, illogically) took his place in the circle. He did not deliberately seek to join it, nor did the magazine purposefully search for him. He gravitated toward it by the same kind of soft and gradual process that sediment settles on the river-bed, while the powerful roar of the water passes over it. Ross wanted to create a weekly review whose interests and humor would appeal to sophisticated inhabitants of a city which had now attained worldly maturity. "Of course Henry James had little or no sense of humor, and in any case did not want to live in the United States, least of all New York. But had he known how to laugh, and been forced to live in Manhattan, this magazine would have appealed to him." Now, this was not Thurber at all. As he once remarked, "There were no opportunities to become sophisticated where I came from." But he could stumble into sophistication, sometimes, where other, more knowing, people would plunge into the yawning pit of banality. He came from a very superstitious family. His mother, in particular, believed in a lot of weird things, though not in the obvious weird things, like God, etc. She believed, for instance, that electricity was dripping out of the sockets, all over the house. She had an invented scientism which made technology seem highly dangerous in all kinds of unexpected ways. She rubbed some of this off on Thurber, so that he tended to anthropomorphize machines, such as cars.

There was also a distinct feeling in the house where he grew up that men and women were in a natural state of warfare with each other. He inherited, and built upon, this feeling, so that it acquired an organic life of its own. Now that fitted in very well with the *New Yorker*. If it was about anything, and of course it wasn't, except about being sophisticated, it was about the war between the sexes. Just as *Punch*, founded in London in the early 1840s, was about (essentially) the war between the classes—we will come to this in the next chapter— so the *New Yorker* dealt with the ways in which men and women, brought up to be kind to each other in the Judeo-Christian tradition, fought for supremacy, to some extent outside marriage, but chiefly within it. It was about many other things too—especially about money, its acquisition and dispersion—but the sex war was its unifying theme, which held it together.

Thurber fitted into this matrix. He was aggressive, especially when drunk, or somewhat in liquor, and found war congenial. Or perhaps one should say he liked the accoutrements and incidentals of warfare: threats and ultimata, provocative assertions and casus belli, zones of influence and protective spaces, the *ballon d'essai* and the *coup diplomatique*. He liked the reality of these concepts but also their nomenclature. On the occasion I met him, we happened to discuss Soviet policy in Southeast Asia, and I quoted Talleyrand as saying "Nonintervention is a metaphysical concept, indistinguishable in practice from intervention." He said, "I guess that's true, and well said. I wish I had said that." He did say, "Someone should apply the principles of Moltke on strategy to the dealings between men and women." He added, "I would like to know the sexual equivalent of the Schlieffen Plan." He began to write for the *New Yorker*, contributing over the years a (for him) substantial number of pieces. Some must be accounted masterpieces of humor. They include: "The Night the Bed Fell," "The Night the Ghost Got In," "The Day the Dam Broke," and "The Secret Life of Walter Mitty." These tales, based upon episodes or moods he half-remembered in real life (insofar as he had a real life) had hints of antagonism between the sexes, or unusual, indeed extraordinary, propensities of one or other in both sexes, and witnessed in his usual cloudy way.

Thurber never saw things quite straight, or remembered them quite straight, and when a blurred obscurity of vision, in the first place, is nebulously recalled, many years later, the result is an unconscious exercise in creative imagination. That can produce humor. Thurber once, in 1960, defined humor as "emotional chaos recollected in tranquility." This was an adaptation of Wordsworth's preface to *Lyrical Ballads* (1798), and it would have been more accurate if Thurber had replaced "recollected" with "rearranged."

Still, he was onto a good point, and it was certainly true that of the two basic types of humor, he dealt in the chaotic one. The term "tranquility" had a very special meaning, however. It signified placid serenity in a way that someone classified officially as a dangerous lunatic can be said to be placid and serene. Harold Ross understood Thurber's prose, at least up to a certain level. Ross seemed to know very little. Many facts which others took for granted came to him as revelations. This was also true of Kingsley Martin, the great editor of the *New Statesman*, and having worked under Martin, and having explained many obvious things to him, and watched his growing delight at acquiring a trivial piece of information no one had hitherto bothered about much, and the use he would make of it, I came to recognize this propensity as the sign of a first-class editor. Ross and Thurber saw each other through a mist, or rather two different mists. Ross saw that what Thurber wrote was funny, in a way he could not understand but which other people would be induced to find funny when they saw it on a *New Yorker* page. This was a mystery to him because he had got it into his head that Thurber was an editorial efficiency expert, and that he ought to be the paper's production editor—indeed, for some years tried to make him do this job. His decision to publish Thurber's stories was skeptical, but it seemed to work. Moreover, he saw that Thurber was fighting the sex war to which the *New Yorker* seemed to be devoted (he did not know why), albeit it was Thurber's own version of the sex war. Thurber's success as a writer he did not understand, as it worried him, inducing him to utter his favorite expression: "How I pity me!"

However, Ross accepted that Thurber's pieces were funny, and familiarity made him laugh at them himself, more particularly since they accorded with a principle he had learned from experience, that humor was often accidental. It was how, to some extent, he ran the paper. What he did not realize, at first, was how large a role accident played in Thurber's life and career. Thurber was lucky that, quite by accident, he shared an office with E. B. White. A New Yorker educated at Cornell, White was a genuine sophisticate, and a rational man whose approach to humor, unlike Ross's, was intellectual not instinctive. Despite his poor sight, Thurber had always liked drawing. It was a release for him from worries, fear, and impotence. As a draftsman he had no gift except one: he was consistently bad. He could not, for instance, draw a woman's legs. So dresses had to come right down to the ankles, which might give the figure a strange significance. And if he drew a woman with her dress hitched up, exposing a bit of leg, it had the eroticism it would have aroused in the eighteenth century. All his figure drawing was bad in this sense. Dorothy Parker said Thurber figures were "unbaked cookies," looking as if made of dough. But they were consistently so, the first step toward style.

Thurber, while thinking—or possibly while not thinking— had the habit of drawing on the lined yellow foolscap the *New Yorker* issued as copy paper. One day he did a scene of a seal on a rock looking at two dots. There was a caption: "H'm. Explorers." White saw it, and loved it: "That's funny. Ink it in." Thurber did so, "my hand shaking." Not from excitement but from worry he would spoil whatever it was White saw in the drawing. White took the drawing to the weekly art conference, where it produced no effect at all. Afterward, Rea Irvin, the art editor, drew a "proper" seal on the same yellow copy paper, and sent it back to White, writing, "This is the way a seal's whiskers go." White persisted. He gave Thurber a lesson on art, and stopped him trying to do shading and hatching. "Look," he said, "if you ever got good, you'd be mediocre." He praised Thurber's drawing to Ross, who was unimpressed. He had Thurber in: "Whatever persuaded you that you could draw. I want you to write, not draw, for Godsake." All this was in the spring of 1929.

White rationalized that Thurber was unconsciously a comic artist of genius, and that his naïveté was the source of his humor. His limitations as a draftsman were precisely his strength. White had written a comic book, *Is Sex Necessary?*, and he got Thurber to illustrate it. It was published in 1929, and quickly sold fifty thousand copies. Some reviewers seemed to feel that the illustrations were very funny and made the book work. This posed a problem for Ross. Was it true that Thurber's drawings were the secret of the book's success? If so: "How I pity me!" The phrase was heard more frequently by the end of 1930 and he had Thurber in. "I want to see that seal drawing again. Bring it to me." "I haven't got it. It was thrown away." Ross was furious. "Don't throw things away just because I reject them. *Do it again*." Thurber was hurt, and refused. Or maybe he thought he couldn't do it again. But in December 1931 he had another try. He found he could not do the seal sitting on a rock. But he could do it sitting on the head of a bed. So, instead of the explorers as dots in the distance, he put a married couple in the bed. This time, the caption took up the sex-war theme, with an angry wife saying to an obstinate husband, "All right, have it your way. You heard a seal bark." The cartoon was published on 30 January 1932 and was an instant success. It was reprinted more than any other twentieth-century cartoon. Timeless, classless, priceless, colorless, it made people laugh in China, India, Africa, South America, and Russia, as well as in Europe. The result of a series of accidents, it struck a note which resounded across the world of the Great Depression, and still makes people laugh in the twenty-first century.

There were other instances in which Thurber's difficulties with drawing accidentally produced a joke which became a classic. The case of the man who introduced a visitor to his first wife, perched or crouched on the top of a bookcase, arose because Thurber, who could not draw some things at all, could draw bookcases, which appear more often than other items of furniture, sometimes inappropriately, and here made the joke. This one baffled Dorothy Parker, who thought the woman was stuffed. But she is obviously alive. Parker was approaching the Thurber joke in the wrong spirit—with logic and reason. But in Thurber's form of chaos humor, logic and reason are not so much abolished as suspended; they are invoked, partly or temporarily, only if needed. Then there is the case of the horse/moose. Thurber's original motive in drawing this animal is not clear. But he found it fitted in well with a feature he was then in charge of, "Our Pet Department," consisting of questions and answers. A reader asked if the drawing was of a moose. If so, there was something wrong with it. Thurber replied that the drawing was of a horse, with a moose's antlers strapped on. In fact, he had put the drawing, in its original form, in his pocket. It was then clearly a moose. It was his habit to have various drawings in his pocket, so that, if he went to a party, he could give a drawing to a floozy he fancied, in return for a feel. On this occasion he went to a drunken party, became drunk himself, and offered the drawing to a drunken woman. She took the drawing, drew teeth on the moose, making it more like a horse, and handed it back. Next morning, Thurber, whose memory of the incident was unclear, wrote the reply to the reader, and published the drawing as altered.

Some of Thurber's more significant drawings dealt directly with the war between the sexes, and some by implication.

There is one of a frightened man returning home to find his wife's enormously enlarged, and angry, features have become the dominant part of the house, so that wife and house have become interchangeable in fact, as they always have been in metaphor. This drawing evolved from Thurber's failure to draw the house, until he perceived it could be changed into the wife, at least in part. His most explicit joke about the sex war is "The Fight in the Grocery Store," in which the women form a team to bombard the men with tins of soup, beans, etc. If Thurber had been a more accomplished artist, he could never have attempted such a complicated subject. As it is, he gets away with it, brilliantly: all the figures are "badly drawn," but they are badly drawn in the same way. It is notable that the women are winning, although they are outnumbered by the men nine to six. This accorded with Thurber's view that women were by nature more aggressive than men, and successfully so. Thus the women are on top; the men servile, silent, or in secret revolt, like Walter Mitty. In the bookcase joke, the man is superficially masterful; yet the first wife is, literally, on top of the bookcase, alive and ready to resume hostilities, possibly in alliance with the second wife.

The sex wars moved imperceptibly in a Thurber drawing into the world of animals. Over the fireplace in the drawing room belonging to Thurber's grandfather was a photograph of the hounds with which "Bendor," the famous Duke of Westminster, used to hunt boar on his estate in France. These dogs left a lifelong impression on Thurber's mind and vision, though he was confused about what kind of dogs they were. Bloodhounds? Basset hounds? No matter. As he rendered them, from memory, they became the archetypal Thurber dog. Three other kinds of animals interested Thurber because he felt he could draw them. He did a large hippolike figure, like a bookcase, with no books but with rounded corners on its oblong shape, and thick legs/feet. If necessary it could be turned into a rhino by adding a triangular horn. This beast became the villain of Thurber's drawing, confronted by an angry woman who, observing bits of male property or attire scattered about, asks, "What have you done with Mr. Millmoss?" A second animal he liked was a kangaroo, which he could draw, after a fashion—well enough to be recognizable anyway. This gave him a formidable courtroom joke, of a kangaroo in the witness-box and a prosecuting council who has just, unexpectedly, "called" the beast, asking the accused, "Perhaps this will refresh your memory." Finally, Thurber liked rabbits: easy to draw, and suggestive of various lines of thought. A rabbit takes the place of the psychiatrist in his anti-woman drawing: "You say, madam, that everyone looks to you like a rabbit?"

The woman looks terrified. Terror, bewilderment, dumb apathy, plus anger, of course, were the expressions Thurber was confident he could convey. He also drew a species of sardonic devilry, as in the case of the cockney butler, somewhat inebriated, who is telling the master of the house, "You see, Sir, we're 'aving a bit of a time downstairs." This was Thurber's only incursion into the English preserve of the class war. Thurber was pleased with this joke because it gave him another chance to draw a bookcase—a handsome antique one too. Sex-war cartooning proved so successful that the *New Yorker* used the heading "The war between men and women" for a whole series, between 20 January and 28 April 1934. Some Thurber drawings were so elusive that they did not fit directly into the sex-war category, yet nonetheless underlined the differences between the sexes. Thus his famous wine snob joke ("It's a naïve domestic Burgundy without any breeding, but I think you'll be amused by its presumption") is spoken, and could only have been spoken (then, anyway: 27 March 1937), by a man. Equally, in his joke "Well, if I called the wrong number, why did you answer the phone?," the remark was made, and could only have been made, by a woman. From time to time, Thurber came out with it, and made his women openly aggressive. Thus the tousle-haired girl who says to the man, "Have you forgotten our little suicide pact?" And the girl who says, "The best fall out of three, OK, Mr. Montague?"

It was once fashionable to compare Thurber's draftsmanship to Picasso's. The similarity is superficial, however. Picasso could draw better than he usually chose to do. Thurber could not. On the other hand, whereas you cannot explain why a Picasso drawing is a masterpiece, in Thurber's case you can. It was also fashionable, in the thirties, to say that Thurber was Matisse's favorite American artist. In 1937, however, Matisse's secretary denied it: "*Le maître* knows nothing of Thurber." All the same, it is recorded that in 1946 when Matisse was asked to name the best artist in the United States, he replied, "Monsieur Toubay." Asked to spell it, he eventually wrote down "Thurber."

It would be untrue to say that the sex war intruded at the *New Yorker* itself, since Ross did not approve of fornication among the regular staff or contributors, on or off the premises, and the women were often not attractive anyway, with the exception of Dorothy Parker. On the other hand, there was a continuous war of, and among, the cartoonists. Every Tuesday, later changed to Wednesday, there was a meeting, presided over by Ross, at which the cartoons for the next issue were chosen. They were often submitted as "roughs," in pencil on tracing paper, and these ideas, if approved, were then done as finished cartoons, usually in India ink on bristol or ivory board. Thanks to Ross, these meetings sometimes lasted five hours, since he needed to have things explained to him. He had the final verdict on whether a cartoon was accepted or not, and he also reserved the right to tell a cartoonist how his drawing could be improved, clarified, or made funnier. He did not usually do this directly but transmitted his orders in memos dictated to his assistant, Miss Terry. Many of these have been preserved. For instance, he would ask, "Which elephant is talking?" Or say, "That's not a butler. That's a banker." Some of his commands were strange and not easy to carry out. Thus: "Reduce the speaker in size, and make him concave." Or: "Better dust" (of a country road). Thurber, once his cartoons became famous, bitterly resented Ross's criticisms, or some of them. There survives an anti-Ross cartoon of his, showing himself, bewildered and resentful, and Ross, drawn as an ugly, angry woman, handing him back a rejected drawing, and saying, "The funny picture is rejected because you can't tell who is talking, the old lady or the fireman, and because we already had a picture of a man trying to get a drink at a dam. Besides, how did the old lady get through the police lines?"

In the light of Ross's limitations, and also his prudery, it is surprising that some of the best *New Yorker* cartoonists of his time ever established themselves on the magazine. Peter Arno, for instance, a highly sophisticated young gentleman, a dropout from Yale and a habitué of Manhattan nightclubs and other forms of life with which Ross was unfamiliar, specialized in couplings of rich men and chorus girls, and similar tricky subjects. Arno had a powerful line, a superb skill with washes (like Rowlandson), and a rich delight in female legs, bosoms, and rears, though avoiding nudity itself. His drawings tended to be risqué, by the standards of the twenties and thirties—or any standards, for that matter. Ross flatly refused to run a brilliant drawing of a couple in bed, the man asleep and snoring away, and the woman yelling at him, "Wake up, you mutt! We're getting married today!" Yet Ross agreed to publish, or was conned into it by an "explanation," a more daring Arno cartoon showing a man in bed between a husband and wife, and saying, "Awfully nice of you to ask me to stay." The wife's face has a lascivious look, which Ross may have missed or misinterpreted. He also ran an Arno cartoon of an orgiastic party with a little boy complaining to his mother, "Mama, there's a lot of people in my bed!" A characteristically memorable Arno drawing, emblematic of the sex-war theme, has a man plunking his busty girlfriend on a bar stool and saying to the bartender, "Fill 'er up!"

Two other important contributors whose tolerance by Ross is mysterious were Charles Addams and Saul Steinberg. Addams was another superb draftsman and wash expert, but his gruesome and sometimes subtle morbidity was not exactly to Ross's taste. Many Addams cartoons had to be explained to him before he agreed to run them, with many a "How I pity me!" Addams became world famous, and was finally dropped by Ross's humorless successor as editor, William Shawn, when the cartoonist's family of monsters went on TV. Ross's ability to accept Steinberg is even stranger, for Steinberg came from Romania and did not arrive in America until 1940. He did not so much draw joke cartoons as visualize thought processes, in a highly idiosyncratic way, never seen before or since, combining Kafka, Paul Klee, and Raoul Dufy. Ross's willingness to allow Steinberg his head is hugely to his credit: one of the best things in his editorship.

Thurber approved of these three artists, each in his own way a comic genius like himself. He approved of Arno despite the fact that he could not always produce his own ideas, and paid professional gag writers to suggest them, something Thurber disliked intensely. But while these three were beyond criticism, Thurber often hated the work of other regulars, especially after liquor, and most particularly when Ross had criticized or refused to run one of his own drawings. There survives in the *New Yorker* archives a furious letter Thurber wrote to Ross in 1937 in which he "demanded" the reconsideration and acceptance of one of his drawings. It continued:

> If this drawing is not funny, and is not a swell drawing, I shall engage to eat it, and with it all of Price's fantasies that just miss, all of Taylor S. Klein's women, and all of eleven versions of every drawing Day does of two men in a restaurant. I shall also eat every drawing of a man and a woman on a raft, every drawing of a man and a native woman on a desert island, and every drawing of two thin women in big-backed chairs. . . . I shall also eat every drawing of a small animal talking to its parents, and every drawing of two large animals talking about their young.

It is notable how many cartoons, by key artists, reached print in the *New Yorker*. Arno, for instance, a contributor from the magazine's founding in 1925 until his death in 1968, produced over one thousand. So did Charles Addams. George Price, an "American Gothic" specialist, who drew his angular human material from his native town of Coytesville, New Jersey, contributed twelve hundred cartoons over sixty years. He was the object of Thurber's particular detestation but did not reciprocate—his hatred being reserved for Norman Rockwell, the *Saturday Evening Post* cover star, who was "in the same racket." Even more cartoons were provided by William Steig, a child artist who had to support his family after the 1929 crash, and worked for the *New Yorker* for over seventy years until his death

in 2003, specializing in children, whom he called "small fry."
In the celebratory volume published by the magazine in 2004,
over two thousand cartoons were republished, and all 68,647
cartoons the magazine had printed in over three quarters of a
century were sent out with the book on disk.

It is surprising how many out of this huge quantity of
cartoons for an adult publication dealt with animals, usually
anthropomorphized in some way. These ranged from a giraffe
saying to a hippo, "Speak up! How can you expect me to hear
you?" and a polar bear pup to its parents, "I don't care what
you say, I'm cold," to two moles in a tunnel, "I backed up the
last time," and two rabbits, "Of course we could adopt some."
There was also a cat saying "No!" to food in a dish marked
"Try It!" and one bee saying to another, "If they knew what
really went on in hives, they'd never eat honey again."

Dorothy Parker used to say, "What I really object to in the
*New Yorker*, or in real life for that matter, is a witty animal."
Like stage actors, and movie actors still more so, she regarded
animals as unfair competition. She usually had a dog, though,
but then, "It knows its place!" Parker, like Thurber, and so
many others, found the burden of professional humor too
heavy to carry eventually, and needed the support and comfort
of heaving drinking. So her life, like his, was sad in the end,
and often in the middle too. What jester's is not? But in its
time, particularly in the twenties, when she was the only pretty
woman who regularly attended the lunchtime "round table"
in the Algonquin Hotel, her flame burned brightly. Much has
been written about the Algonquin round tables, and much is

exaggerated or apocryphal about the sallies and laughter, but a contemporary painting of the regulars, commissioned by Paul Hyde Banner, shows Parker with George S. Kaufman, Alexander Woollcott, Harpo Marx, Heywood Brown, Robert Benchley, Irving Berlin, and various others—including a characteristically glum and puzzled Harold Ross—all skilled, and usually successful, in raising a laugh.

Parker had wit in that special American form, the one-liner. Nobody except Mark Twain coined so many, all mint. Many are in rhyme, of a sort. Thus:

Men seldom make passes
At girls who wear glasses.

Or

Guns aren't lawful.
Nooses give.
Gas smells awful
You might as well live.

Or

Why is it no one ever sent me yet
One perfect limousine, do you suppose?
Ah no, it's always just my luck to get
One perfect rose.

Or

By the time you say you're his
Shivering and sighing,
And he vows his passion is
Infinite, undying.
Lady, make note of this
One of you is lying.

Parker's wit sprang from her sardonic nature, and her delight in words. From her address to the American Horticultural Society: "You can lead a horticulture, but you can't make her think." To the staff of *Vogue*: "Brevity is the soul of lingerie, as the petticoat said to the chemise." On her abortion: "Serves me right for putting all my eggs in one bastard." To Harold Ross: "Wit has truth in it. Wisecracking is simply calisthenics with words." On Los Angeles: "Seventy-two suburbs in search of a city." Epitaph for herself: "Excuse my dust." Abrasions: "Scratch a lover and find a foe." "Scratch an actor and find an actress." To a friend who went to the country to have her baby: "Congratulations. We knew you had it in you." On a story by Hugh Walpole: "This is not a novel to be tossed aside lightly. It should be thrown with great force." Parker had no illusions. A great partygoer, she might exclaim, when the door opened to reveal a scene of crowded revelry: "What fresh hell is this?" Liquor she enjoyed, and feared:

I love a dry martini,
But one or two at most.
After three, I'm under the table
Four, I'm under my host.


Wit should be cut to the bone, she said. So she called Alexander Woollcott's Manhattan apartment "Wit's end." And for her tombstone she wrote her own epitaph: "This is on me."

The *New Yorker*, and the people to whom it gave opportunities to display their humorous skills, probably made more sophisticated, English-speakers laugh than any other institution in the twentieth century. And that is odd, because the man who created it, and ran it until it *became* an institution, was wholly unsophisticated. He had edited, for years, the *American Legion Weekly*. Parker, who knew him long before he started the *New Yorker*, said he had thought, and talked a lot, about starting a shipping paper, to be called the *Marine Gazette*. She said, "He was almost illiterate." He was a wild man who "never read anything and didn't know anything." She said, "His ignorance was of Grand Canyon dimensions, so deep you had to admire it for its sheer size." He was "a monolith of unsophistication." But in that mysterious way humor works, he created a fine instrument of humorous art, and that was the biggest joke of all.

CHAPTER FOURTEEN

# NOËL COWARD, NANCY MITFORD, AND CLASS

I F THE WAR between the sexes provided the biggest single source of humor among educated Americans, as an analysis of the content of the *New Yorker* jokes indicates, the English equivalent was the class war. A similar analysis of two thousand cartoons in *Punch*, from its foundation in 1841 until 1992, gives jokes about class the lead, though animals, sports, and sex warfare run it close. On close inspection, "class war" is the wrong term, unless used with a touch of irony. The civil war of the 1640s was the last occasion the classes took to serious violence in England, and religion, and the right to tax, played at least as prominent a role in setting it off as class. "Class skirmishing" is probably a more accurate description of what went on and provided ideas for jokes.

More important, the chief source of humor was not the class system itself, and its rigidity, but precisely its flexibility,

and the opportunities for satire, irony, and buffoonery provided by upward mobility. There were certain social concepts which developed deep in English history, and provided
food for humorous feasts as far back as the fourteenth century, giving Chaucer, for instance, wonderful material for his
*Canterbury Tales*. "Pushy," "getting above himself," "uppity,"
"bounders," "counter-jumpers"—such phrases, or rather the
phenomena they represent, are very ancient, stretching back to
the Middle Ages, and were reinforced, fresh colored, updated,
and envenomed with each new generation. Furthermore, it is
a key fact that the writers and artists who made best use of the
class joke were themselves, in almost every case, instances of
upward mobility. Chaucer made himself thoroughly at home
in courts but was actually the son of a wine merchant. Shakespeare's father sold gloves; William Congreve's was a professional soldier; Richard Brinsley Sheridan's an actor-manager;
Jane Austen's a parish clergyman and schoolteacher; Dickens's
an insolvent clerk in the Navy Office.

If we look at the English (or, if you like, British) comedy
of class in the twentieth century, the same principle applies.
Of the successful practitioners, only the Hon. Nancy Mitford
(1904–1973) was the daughter of a peer, and he succeeded
to the title comparatively late in life after some unsuccessful
commercial adventures in the empire. The rest were all middle
class, in its infinite gradations from lower lower to fairly upper.
A typical example was Graham Laidler, known as "Pont,"
the great star of *Punch* in the 1930s, whose series of over

one hundred cartoons, "The British Character"—essentially a genial satire on the possessing/ruling class—made him a major comic artist, in the Hogarth-Rowlandson category. Pont came from the Newcastle area, the least salubrious, from a class viewpoint, of the provinces; he was the son of a businessman and, when he first came to London, had a distinctive Geordie accent. H. M. Bateman, who thrived on his cartoons of shocking social behavior and solecisms, especially "things that are *not done*," such as "The Man who Threw a Snowball at St. Moritz," came from right outside the English class hierarchy. He was born in New South Wales, son of a farmer, never went near an English public school or Oxbridge, and had an Australian accent to his dying day.

The outstanding case of upper-class fantasy woven by a middle-class archetype was P. G. Wodehouse. His father was a stipendiary magistrate in Hong Kong. He was brought up by uncles and aunts in Bath and Croydon, the latter a suburban capital of middle-class respectability, and his public school, Dulwich, though ancient and excellent (it also produced Raymond Chandler, the Chekhov of Los Angeles), was far from fashionable. He escaped Oxbridge by going to work for the Hong Kong and Shanghai Bank. It is true he was distantly related to the earls of Kimberly, and given the grand-sounding forenames of Pelham and Grenville. But he did not use them, and they adorned the title page only of his first novel, *Something Fresh* (1915). Thereafter he wrote as P. G. Wodehouse. In an autobiographical passage he recalled:

If you ask me to tell you frankly if I like the names Pelham Grenville, I must confess I do not. . . . At the font I remember protesting vigorously when the clergyman uttered them, but he stuck to his point. "Be that as it may," he said firmly, having waited for a lull, "I name thee Pelham Grenville."

The fact that Wodehouse, thoroughly middle class, was imaginatively ennobled in nomenclature, was doubtless a key to his construction, as a writer, of an entirely imaginary upper-class England, which never existed and never could exist, inhabited by aristocratic inventions of his own. To make matters more complex, Wodehouse was by choice an Anglo-American hybrid, who spent much of his early adult life in Manhattan, seeking to write Broadway musicals. When he married, his wife had $75 and he had $60, and they were rescued by George Horace Lorimer, editor of the *Saturday Evening Post*, who bought *Something Fresh* as a serial for "the stupefying sum of $3,500, at that time the equivalent of seven hundred gleaming golden sovereigns." In the twenties Wodehouse was more often in New York than in London; in the thirties he lived chiefly in Le Touquet, whence he was deported by the Nazi invaders to Germany, was naively indiscreet, and, therefore, after the Second World War, forced to live outside England again. It is therefore anomalous, though characteristically so, that this dislocated middle-class epigone should have produced 120 novels exploiting the opportunities presented by the English class system for aristocratic hilarity.

NOËL COWARD, NANCY MITFORD . . .    197

A still more striking case is Noël Coward (1899–1973). He got even more comic mileage out of English class differentials than Wodehouse, who after all was not a satirist, let alone a savage one, but a fabricator of harmless fairy tales about the landed interest. And Coward was born into the genteel poverty of suburban Teddington. His father was a piano salesman, not of grands either, or even baby grands, but of lower-middle-class uprights. Born in 1899 he entered showbiz at the earliest possible moment and became, in his own words, "a brazen, odious little prodigy," though his earnings could not save his mother from taking in lodgers. His first professional appearance, aged twenty, was in 1911, and by 1920 he was an old hand at every aspect of the theater, rising through *Peter Pan*, *Charley's Aunt*, singing, dancing, filming, the company of Charles Hawtrey, "who taught me character-acting," writing his own songs, scripts, a novel or two, and plays. In the early 1920s he made himself the hit comedy playwright of the London stage with *The Young Idea* (1922), *The Vortex* and *Hay Fever* (1924), and *Fallen Angels* (1925). By 1925 he was a top London celebrity who knew everyone from the Prince of Wales to the governor of the bank.

By now he had a cut-glass Mayfair-Oxford accent, and was up to all the tricks of the sophisticated rich and well born. But note: he taught himself all this in the rough and tumble of Shaftesbury Avenue, well before he got the entrée to Mayfair drawing rooms. A top comedy actor had to possess an upper-class accent. He told me, "It's easy to downgrade it into plebs but not the other way round. Your posh speech has to be real.

You have to think your soul into the body of a rich young man-about-town, with a valet, who belongs to Brooks's or White's, the Royal Enclosure at Ascot, calls Lady Cunard 'Emerald,' Lord Birkenhead 'FE,' and Lord Beaverbrook 'Max'!" "How did you do it, then?" "Clothes, old boy. Essentially clothes. Once you got the clothes right, and they had to be dead right, and made yourself feel at home in them—easy for a professional actor—all the rest followed. I bought my first dinner jacket, tails and morning suit second-hand—I was a teenager. But once I had a hit, I went to Leslie & Roberts. 'The trouser should shiver on the shoe, but should not break'—I remember old Roberts saying that to me. When I first went through the door at Lady Colefax's in my new Savile Row suit, I knew I was going to make it."

Soon Coward was giving advice to other upstarts, like the rising photographer Cecil Beaton: "Your sleeves are too tight—your voice is too high and too precise. You mustn't do it, my dear. It closes so many doors. . . . It's hard, I know. One would like to indulge one's own taste. I myself dearly love a good match, yet I know it's overdoing it to wear tie, socks and handkerchief in the same color. I take ruthless stock of myself in the mirror before going out. By the way, don't say 'mirror,' say 'looking-glass.'"

The between-the-wars period, the last time when people, especially men, were judged by their clothes, was the grand climacteric of sartorial fashion. George Bernard Shaw wrote, "Acquired notions of propriety are stronger than natural instincts. It is easier to recruit for monasteries and convents than to induce a British officer [in mufti] to walk through Bond Street in a golfing cap in May." A desperate rearguard action was fought to compel theater audiences in the stalls, especially at first nights, to wear full evening dress of white tie, tails, and top hat. A correspondence in *The Times* in 1932 reflected indignation at the "new breed" of "middle class theatre-goers" daring to sit in the stalls wearing dinner jackets instead of white tie and tails. It was "very distressing," wrote one correspondent, "for any who have paid for their stalls and taken the trouble to don evening dress . . . to find themselves seated next to persons still wearing the same clothes they have worked in all through the day." Another correspondent, from the other side of the sartorial class barrier, confessed he found himself "uncomfortable" as "the only man in the stalls that night in a grey tweed suit . . . a fitting subject for H. M. Bateman." Anger was expressed that the "worst dressed" stalls were to be found at plays by Shakespeare and Shaw.

King George V, like his father Edward VII, who addressed an incorrectly dressed duke at the Ascot races, "Hello, Devonshire, going ratting?," was a fanatic for correct dress. Clothes were the only subject on which he could bear to talk to his eldest son, later Edward VIII, later still Duke of Windsor, whom he despised as idle and frivolous. They would sit uneasily together, discussing such topics as trouser turnups, whether trousers should be creased at the front or side (on both of which they disagreed furiously), and how a cravat or necktie should be tied. George V thoroughly disapproved of his son's invention, or popularization, of a method which became known as "the Windsor knot." George V also rowed with the second son, later King George VI, for wearing khaki shorts when he attended a summer camp for poor city boys which he patronized. It was "damned bad form." Not only kings rowed over clothes. Fred Astaire, who did his best to keep the flag flying for faultless evening dress, in such movies as *Top Hat*, put in a scene in which his British producer and valet had a dispute between the "square-ended" and the butterfly bow tie.

Attention, and jokes, also centered on other sartorial blunders. It was "the height of caddishness" (George V again) to wear brown shoes, and still more brown boots, "in town" (i.e., in London). There was a famous music hall song, "Brahn Boots" (1910), later sung by Stanley Holloway (the comic cockney star of *My Fair Lady*):

> And we could hear the neighbours all remark,
> "Wot? 'Im, chief mourner? Wot a bloomin lark!
> Why, 'ee looks more like a bookmaker's clerk
> In brahn boots!"

Footwear was regarded as a class giveaway. In 1922 *Punch* complained that office boys were aping "their betters" by wearing spats. "Where will it all end?" the magazine moaned. Spats were also demonized as the sign of a seducer of young women. A seaside postcard declared, "A white spat may often hide the cloven hoof." By the end of the twenties, in London, sure signs of a "vulgar cad" were said to be spats, lemon-colored gloves, double-breasted waistcoats, bowler hats, and overcoats described as "overdone." Brown suede shoes were the mark of homosexuals (and were frowned upon in Buckingham Palace until well into the reign of Elizabeth II). Two-toned shoes for men were known as corespondents and, when worn by the Duchess of Windsor, were hailed as "proof positive she is an adulteress." Respectable people would not buy such footwear. For more information about such matters, readers should consult a brilliant and deeply researched survey by the clothes historian Catherine Horwood, *Keeping Up Appearances: Fashion and Class between the Wars.*

From our present-day perspective, we are amazed by how many different articles of clothing people with any kind of social pretensions possessed in those days. In Evelyn Waugh's unfinished novel *Work Suspended,* set on the eve of the Second World War, the hero, temporarily homeless in London, is worried chiefly because he has nowhere to keep his hats.

I owned what now seems a multitude of them, of one sort or another; two of them of silk—the tall hat I took to weddings, and a second hat bought some years earlier when I thought for a time I was going to take to fox hunting. There was a bowler; a panama; a black, a brown, and a gray soft hat; a green hat for Salzburg; a sombrero; some tweed caps for use onboard ships and on trains— all these had accumulated from time to time and all, with the possible exception of the sombrero, were more or less indispensable.

There were also arguments not only about when to wear hats, and what hats to wear, but when to raise them or take them off outright. Hat etiquette was by no means confined to the upper classes. George Orwell, in *The Road to Wigan Pier*, noted that in the 1920s, in northern industrial towns, not wearing a hat in the street was a sign of disrespect for society as a whole, and a hatless man was liable to be stoned by street urchins. You need not take off your hat in a shop, but must do so in a doctor's surgery, and a lawyer's office. A bank was a marginal case. The *Hatter's Gazette*, a mine of information on etiquette, warned, "A man who does not keep his hat on in a department store may be treated as a floor-walker."

The cartoonist Pont, whose "normal" characters tended to dress for dinner, in black tie at home, in white tie when "going out," was very careful about hats, a sure means to distinguish between a proper Englishman and a "foreign person" or, worse, an intellectual. Even more careful was the cartoonist Osbert Lancaster, whose work between the 1920s and his retirement and death toward the close of the twentieth century is a detailed and infallible guide to prevailing fashions and certitudes in dress. For instance, in his superb drawing of the Café Royal and its habitués in the 1930s, he carefully distinguishes between writers and intellectuals who kept their hats on, and those who did not. In the huge cast of characters he assembled in this one drawing—Evelyn Waugh, Hannen Swaffer the columnist, Cecil Beaton the photographer, Cyril Connolly and Peter Quennell, critics, Kingsley Martin the left-wing editor, Lord David Cecil the fashionable don, Victor Gollancz the publisher, Lord Berners the society aesthete, Constant Lambert the composer, Brian Howard and Tom Driberg the society homosexuals, Sheila Kaye-Smith, Barbara Skelton, Olivia Manning, and Marghanita Laski the literary ladies and molls, James Agate the theater critic, and Kenneth Clark the art expert—Lancaster gave a visual and topographical perspective of the London intelligentsia which no photographer could supply. He did a similar personal panorama of Glyndebourne, the fashionable privately owned opera house, where patrons are still expected to "change" for the performance. And for more than half a century Lancaster produced "pocket cartoons," mainly for the *Daily Express*, which gave accurate shape, especially in dress, hats, hair, beards and moustaches, handbags, medals, and accessories of every kind, of all the groups which gave spice and flavor to London society, from cabinet ministers and demagogues, dukes, earls, and nouveaux riches life peers, talkative clergymen and reticent civil servants, army and navy chiefs, and visiting American firemen, intellectuals, movie stars, and pop singers, and indeed everyone who briefly took a place in the daily newspaper hall of transient fame. It remains a great achievement in the English comic tradition, beautifully commemorated in a retrospect volume, *Cartoons and Coronets: The Genius of Osbert Lancaster*, compiled by James Knox.

What Pont and Osbert Lancaster did in cartoons, Noël Coward put on the stage. It is a matter of dispute who was the greatest humorist on the English scene in the twentieth century, but Noël Coward was, and is, a strong contender for the title, not least because he lived and wrote for so much of it, and because he made memorable jokes in private conversation as well as for public performance. Thus when Godfrey Winn and Beverley Nichols, two notorious lovey-dovey homosexual columnists, played a fatal game of tennis, during which Winn collapsed of a heart attack and died, on court and in mid-match, Coward asked, "Didn't anyone record the score? No matter. I expect it was love-all." And when the mountainous queen of Tonga, the capital of what was once called the Cannibal Islands, attended Elizabeth II's coronation in 1953, a tiny black man in a top hat and morning coat was perched next to her in her carriage. Who was he? Coward was asked (he was actually the local prime minister). "Him?" Coward replied. "That's her lunch." Coward himself, immensely and variously gifted, and always hardworking, had no pretensions to being a genius. In one of his songs from his review *Bitter Sweet*, he sang

> I believe that since my life began
> The most I've had is just
> A talent to amuse.

His ability to concoct funny lyrics, set to catchy tunes, which he wrote himself, came close to genius, as was apparent when he himself sang them. Some have argued that Cole Porter's lyrics were better, and it may be that one or two are— Coward himself was fulsome in praising "Let's Do It (Let's Fall in Love)" as "the perfect light comedy song, as we can all add verses of our own." But Porter's lyric-verse structures were simple, one reason it is so easy to add verses to "Let's Do It." By contrast, Coward often created complicated verse patterns, with tricky rhymes precisely so he could set them to music with unexpected verse endings, whose brilliant effectiveness only emerged when they were sung, especially by himself. There are three examples, chosen from many, which illustrate the point. My own favorite is his hit at the theatrical-lower-middle-class digs milieu: "Don't Put Your Daughter on the Stage, Mrs. Worthington." This was a world he knew well from childhood and youth, loved and hated, and wrote his lines to be well and truly punched. Each verse ended "Don't put your daughter on the stage," and for the last one he added two short lines:

Please, Mrs. Worthington!
On my knees, Mrs. Worthington!
Don't put your daughter on the stage!

The last line sung fortissimo with an orchestral *tutti con brio*. A professional, of course, but gloriously funny when the Master (as he liked to be called) sang, mimed, and danced it.

His most popular lyric of all, "Mad Dogs and Englishmen go out in the Midday Sun," he wrote on "a long drive" in Southeast Asia, in a rickshaw. He wrote it, with its complex verse form, to be sung very fast, but with key pauses. Cole Porter said it was the only song he'd ever heard sung (by Coward himself, of course) in one breath. The variations in the lines are crucial:

Mad dogs and Englishmen
Go out in the midday sun
The toughest Burmese bandit
Can never understand it
In Rangoon, the heat of noon
Is just what the natives shun

"Mad Dogs" is a satire on the English as opposed to the other races, white as well as brown and black. By contrast "The stately homes of England" is a robust dig at the English upper classes, at a time when they were still part of the ruling political and social elite. In many ways it is Coward's most accomplished lyric, sung by four eldest sons bearing the courtesy titles of their houses, a chance for in-jokes. The rules of copyright prevent extensive quotation, more's the pity, or perhaps it is just as well as one is tempted to reproduce the entire song. The lyric is full of delightful variations and tricks, the last verse being particularly cunning with two extra rhymes leading to a fortissimo last line:

If anyone spots the Queen of Scots
In a hand-embroidered shroud
We're proud
Of the stately homes of England.

Noël Coward's talents for comedy added up to a kind of genius, which, on occasion, produced work of such quality, and at such dazzling speed, as to suggest inspiration. During the Second World War he wrote, put on, and acted in *Blithe Spirit*, a satire on spiritualism which turned out to be the funniest play since Oscar Wilde's *The Importance of Being Earnest*. Like that glittering play, it had undertones and overtones of class to add spice to its farce, and it proved the longest-running comedy ever in London until the 1970s. Coward wrote, "I will ever be grateful for the almost psychic gift that enabled me to write *Blithe Spirit* in five days during one of the darkest years of the war."

Coward once referred to the English upper classes as "an inexhaustible source of comedy for a professional humorist like myself." They constituted "a coal mine to be worked—even a salt mine." A fellow worker was the Hon. Nancy Mitford, eldest of the six beautiful daughters of David, 2nd Baron Redesdale. They ran the gamut of views and ambitions. Nancy was mildly left wing and Jessica (or Decca) violently so. Diana was extreme right wing and married the English fascist leader Sir Oswald Mosley, while Unity was ultra-Nazi and fell in love with Hitler. Pam and Deborah (Debo) were social, and Debo spent most of her life as the Duchess of Devonshire. They were all clever and funny but Nancy was the cleverest and wittiest. She was a bad picker of men, and married a man about town named Peter Rodd, in life a prize bore but transformed by Evelyn Waugh into a fascinating fictive cad as Basil Seal. During the war, Nancy got a job as assistant at Heywood Hill's fashionable Mayfair bookshop in Curzon Street, which she ran as a salon where intellectuals with social pretensions, like Osbert Sacherevell, and Edith Sitwell, Waugh, John Betjeman,

Graham Greene, Malcolm Muggeridge, Lord Berners, Driberg, Connolly, and Maurice Bowra, could converge and indulge in what Nancy called "shrieks"—loud, uncontrolled laughter. There was born the idea which emerged as her novel *The Pursuit of Love*, which became a bestseller at the end of the war, at roughly the same time as Waugh's *Brideshead Revisited*. This was based upon the family of Lord Beauchamp, whom Waugh knew well. The earl had married a sister of the Duke of Westminster, the horribly rich and ruthless Bendor, who resented the homosexuality of the man he called "my bugger-in-law," and eventually drove him into exile by threats of police prosecution. The novel combines high and low comedy with tragedy and religious redemption, using the English class system and its customs with masterly skill (Waugh, like Coward, was a social climber of genius, but started from a somewhat higher baseline). It rightly retains its appeal in the twenty-first century. Nancy's novel is pure comedy, based upon her own family and its patriarch, Lord Redesdale, who appears as Uncle Matthew. He is xenophobic ("abroad is perfectly bloody and all foreigners are fiends"), castigates intellectuals as "sewers," and taught his children boisterous games. One such game involved shouting the command "Prepare to receive cavalry," at which he rode his hunter at them as fast as he could, jumping over them at the last minute. Another was "the Child Hunt," his own variation of Hare and Hounds during which he hunted the girls over the countryside with his bloodhounds and a terrier named Luncheon Tom. Uncle Matthew is the superficially frightening but fundamentally amiable antihero of the novel, the real hero being a French lover of the heroine founded on Colonel Gaston Palewski, aide-de-camp to the French resistance leader, General de Gaulle. Nancy was in love with him for the rest of her life, and the huge financial success of *The Pursuit of Love* enabled her to live in Paris, where she could receive his occasional caresses and endure his womanizing and general neglect.

I met her in Paris in the early fifties, after she had written a second bestseller, *Love in a Cold Climate* (this brilliant title was invented for her by Waugh, her literary mentor) and became a celebrated figure in Paris salon society. I call her "Nancy" but in fact she liked to be called Mrs. Rodd, even though she was in the process of getting divorced. She was oddly formal in some ways and a stickler for the conventions, while at the same time laughing at herself. Shortly after I met her she met, at a lunch party, a Birmingham University philological don named A. S. C. Ross. He told her he was writing an article, for the Finnish learned journal called *Neuphilologische Mitteilungen*, on "speech indicators," words and phrases which revealed the class status of the person who used them. He called these words "U" (upper class) and "non-U." Nancy was fascinated, and immediately pounced on the issue for an article she was writing called "The English Aristocracy," which Stephen Spender had persuaded her to write for *Encounter*, the intellectual monthly he edited, in an effort to increase its flagging circulation.

The theory of "class-indicators" in speech was not new, of course. It went back to Shakespeare, indeed Chaucer, whose nun-prioress's pronunciation of French was "after the school of Stratford-atte-Bowe, for French of Paris was to her unknowe." In the postwar world, where the lower-middle classes, now educated at universities (admittedly "redbrick" or even "white-tile" ones, as opposed to "Oxbridge") were pushing up into the ranks of the "upper middles" or even higher, class usage in speech was a good barrier to keep them down. John Betjeman, an assiduous analyst of the English class system in architecture, dress, speech, and mannerisms, had already got on to the point in a poem called "How to Get On in Society." This lists twenty-seven of the words not to be used if you want to shake off your lower-middle-class origins, and its first line is "Phone for the fish-knives, Norman." Phone is non-U—you must say "telephone," and fish-knives, for obscure reasons, are never used by the upper classes, and certainly never referred to as such. Betjeman also listed "serviette" (made of paper) as a non-U abomination, as opposed to napkin, made of linen, the proper U term. Nancy added many others, such as "bike" (U) as opposed to "cycle" (non-U), "writing paper" (U) as opposed to "notepaper" (non-U), and many others.

The article was an immediate success, being quoted in countless magazines and newspapers. *Encounter* sold out and had to be reprinted, the circulation doubled for a time and ensured the precarious magazine another twenty years of life. The terms "U" and "non-U" became part of the English language. See, for instance, the long and learned entries in the *Oxford English Dictionary*. The controversy spread into a dozen books on the subject, such as *Noblesse Oblige*, edited by Nancy herself. It crossed the Atlantic, Ogden Nash pointing out in *You Can't Get There from Here*, "The wicked queen said 'Mirror, mirror on the wall' instead of 'Looking glass, looking glass on the wall'! So the wicked queen exposed herself not only as wicked but definitely non-U." There were arguments. Evelyn Waugh argued that upper-class families always had their personal lists of U and non-U words and expressions. There was no uniformity. Notepaper and writing paper were not alternatives: notepaper, for "notes," writing paper a double sheet, for proper letters. It was also argued that the term "Saturday-to-Monday," the U expression for the non-U "weekend," was now hopelessly out of date, and that weekend was universal, and acceptable. Nancy Mitford herself discovered, to her horror, that her earlier novels *Highland Fling* and *Pigeon Pie*, were full of terms like "mirror" and others she now described as non-U, such as "mantelpiece" and "handbags." She had to correct them in new editions, and begged Waugh, to whom she made this confession, "Don't tell my public, or I'm done for." Of course she had intended the whole thing as a tease, and was flabbergasted (a dubiously non-U expression) when it was taken with deadly seriousness by a great many people and institutions, including both the London *Times* and the *New York Times*. She wailed, "Now I have to think what I'm saying all the time in case I slip into a non-U expression by mistake." The best strategy was to go ahead regardless of such distinctions and assert your social self-confidence by saying what you please.

The central character in Osbert Lancaster's pocket cartoons in the *Daily Express*, Maudie, countess of Littlehampton, took this line. At the height of the uproar, Lancaster drew Maudie Littlehampton spooning into her mouth a knifeful of peas, and exclaiming defiantly, "What I say is, if it's Me, it's U!"

The concept of U speech was the last attempt of the old ruling class in England to define its supremacy against the encroaching "lower orders" (U speech for the proletariat). The attempt has now, in the early twenty-first century, been largely abandoned, as have efforts to insist on certain dress conventions, such as wearing ties in restaurants. Institutions like the Garrick Club, which will not admit men not wearing a tie, either as members or guests, and will not admit women at all as members, now tend to invoke derision rather than command respect. At the Beefsteak Club, which considers itself socially superior to the Garrick, and more exclusive, the verdict is: "What can you expect from a club whose members are mainly actor-fellows and attorneys?" But the Beefsteak has its own U-rules, such as that all waiters must be addressed as Charles, irrespective of their real names, that members must sit for meals at the one big table in the order in which they arrive at the club, and that it is forbidden to ask your neighbor his name. Most non-U prohibitions in speech, such as "mirror" have been scrapped. There are one or two exceptions. When I was a young man in the 1940s, only debutantes used the word "loo" for lavatory. Now it is almost universal except among official labelers, who insist on using "toilet" ("Ladies" and "Gentlemen" having been scrapped as antisocial).

There has, however, over the last generation, arisen a pestilential system known as Political Correctness, which might be described as the response of the underlings to U-usage. It is invented and enforced not by the working class, who are traditionally robust in speech, but by members of the lower-middle classes with official positions and leftish leanings—municipal librarians, state schoolteachers, minor employees in central and local government. It is primarily a system of verbal and written censorship, banning all words and expressions likely to "cause offense"—racist terms, expressions reflecting "ageism." It is now Politically Incorrect, for example, not only to refer to a "cripple" but to describe someone as "in a wheelchair." In an attempt to put down "racism," the concept of "hate terms" was introduced into English law for the first time. This makes many words and expressions unlawful, and punishable by fines and imprisonment. It is the most comprehensive system of censorship since the days of Hitler's Germany and Stalin's Russia, and means that there is more restriction on freedom of expression in England than at any time since Hogarth's day.

It is, of course, fatal to humor, if enforced and persisted in. For one vital element of humor is inequality, and striking visual, aural, and physical differences. Differences in sex, age, color, race, religion, physical ability, and strength lie at the source of probably the majority of jokes since the beginning of human self-consciousness. And all jokes are liable to provoke discomfort if not positive misery among those laughed at. Hence any joke is liable to fall foul of hate laws. The future for humorists thus looks bleak, at the time I write this. The ordinary people like jokes, often crude ones, as George Orwell pointed out in his perceptive essay on rude seaside picture postcards. But are ordinary people, as opposed to minor officials, in charge anymore? Democracy doesn't really seem to work, and people are insufficiently dismayed at its impotence. Noël Coward made the point more than half a century ago:

> There are bad times just around the corner.
> We can all look forward to despair.
> It's as clear as crystal
> From Birmingham to Bristol
> That we can't save democracy
> And we don't much care.

# FURTHER READING

T HE LIFE AND works of Hogarth are examined in
great detail in Ronald Paulson's trilogy, *Hogarth*, Vol. 1,
*The Modern Moral Subject 1697–1732*; Vol. 2, *High Art and
Low 1732–1750*; Vol. 3, *Art and Politics 1750–1764* (New
Brunswick, N.J.: Rutgers University Press, 1991–1993). The
most useful book on Franklin I have read is H. W. Brands,
*The First American: The Life and Times of Benjamin Franklin*
(New York: Doubleday, 2000). The best single-volume life of
Dr. Johnson is Walter Jackson Bate, *Samuel Johnson* (New York
and London: Harcourt Brace Jovanovich, 1977), but for more
detail there is a trilogy by James L. Clifford. I also recommend
the useful little volume *The Sayings of Doctor Johnson*, edited
by Brenda O'Casey (London: Duckworth, 1990). For Rowlandson there is no entirely satisfactory work. Joseph Grego's
pioneering *Rowlandson the Caricaturist*, originally published

in two volumes in 1880 (London: Chatto and Windus), has been reissued by Collectors Editions Ltd. of New York. These volumes should be supplemented by John Hayes, *The Art of Thomas Rowlandson* (Alexandria, Va.: Art Services International, 1990), and by Arthur W. Heintzelman, *The Watercolor Drawings of Thomas Rowlandson*, 2d ed. (New York: Watson-Guptill Publications, 1971). For Dickens, see the Pilgrim edition, *The Letters of Charles Dickens*, edited by Madeline House and Graham Storey, 12 vols. (Oxford: Clarendon Press, 1965–2002). For G. K. Chesterton, see Maisie Ward, *Gilbert Keith Chesterton*, 2d ed. (London: Sheed and Ward, 1944) and *A Motley Wisdom: The Best of G. K. Chesterton*, edited by Nigel Ford (London: Hodder and Stoughton, 1995). The G. K. Chesterton Institute for Faith and Culture at Seton Hall University publishes *The Chesterton Review*, with articles on Chesterton and other pertinent topics, as well as various other works; more information is available at http://www.shu.edu/catholic-mission/chesterton-index.cfm. The best life of Toulouse-Lautrec is by Julia Frey, *Toulouse-Lautrec: A Life* (London: Weidenfeld and Nicolson, 1994); supplemented by the catalog of the exhibition of his work in London and Paris in 1991–1992: *Toulouse-Lautrec: Hayward Gallery, London, 10 October 1991–19 January 1992; Galeries nationals du Grand Palais, Paris, 21 February–1 June 1992* (London: South Bank Centre; Paris: Réunion des musées nationaux, 1991). For Damon Runyon, see his publications *Guys and Dolls* (New York: Stokes, 1932), *Take it Easy* (New York: Stokes, 1938), *Runyon à la Carte* (Philadelphia and New York: Lippincott, 1944), *In Our Town* (New York:

Creative Age Press, 1946), and *Short Takes* (New York and London: Whitlesey House, McGraw-Hill Book Company, 1946). For Thurber, see his autobiographical *The Years with Ross* (Boston: Little, Brown, 1959) and (among his many collections of stories and drawings) *My World—and Welcome to It* (New York: Harcourt, Brace, 1942), *Men, Women and Dogs* (New York: Harcourt, Brace, 1943), *Thurber Carnival* (New York and London: Harper, 1945), *The Beast in Me and Other Animals* (New York: Harcourt, Brace, 1948), and *Thurber Country* (New York: Simon and Schuster, 1953). For Dorothy Parker see Marion Meade, *Dorothy Parker: What Fresh Hell Is This?* (New York: Villard Books, 1987). For silent movies, see Paul Merton, *Silent Comedy* (London: Random House, 2007). For Chaplin see *My Autobiography* (London: Bodley Head, 1964) and Kenneth S. Lynn, *Charlie Chaplin and His Times* (New York: Simon and Schuster, 1997). For Fields see Simon Louvish, *Man on the Flying Trapeze: The Life and Times of W. C. Fields* (London: Faber, 1997). For Laurel and Hardy see Simon Louvish, *Stan and Ollie, The Roots of Comedy: The Double Life of Laurel and Hardy* (London: Faber, 2001). Louvish also wrote the best book on the Marx Brothers, *Monkey Business: The Lives and Legends of the Marx Brothers* (London: Faber, 1999). For Osbert Lancaster, see *Cartoons and Coronets: The Genius of Osbert Lancaster*, edited by James Knox (London: Lincoln, 2008). For Noël Coward see his two volumes of autobiography, *Present Indicative* and *Future Indefinite* (London: Heinemann 1937 and 1954). For Nancy Mitford, see *Love from Nancy: The Letters of Nancy Mitford*, edited by

Charlotte Mosley (London: Hodder and Stoughton, 1993) and Selina Hastings, *Nancy Mitford: A Biography* (London: Hamilton, 1985). For clothes humor, see Catherine Horwood, *Keeping Up Appearances: Fashion and Class between the Wars* (Stroud, U.K.: Sutton, 2005). For Pont see the catalog of the exhibition *Pont: Observing the British at Home and Abroad* held in 2008 at the Cartoon Museum in Holborn, London.

# INDEX